"In *Finding Your Role*, Jacob inspiring readers with the impc and to society. The effectiver. weaves three things together: simple explanation based in Scripture, relatable examples from the world of sports (even relatable to non-sporty people like me), and very practical steps that readers can begin taking right away. In addition to informing and inspiring a broader audience, *Finding Your Role* could function as a useful discipleship tool, especially for youth leaders."

—Travis Arnold, Professor of Theology, Portland Bible College

"Jacob Miller did something a lot of people in their twenties forget to do; he paid attention. You will see what I mean; he has thought deeply about Christ and His church. In a world where "people care more about their following than who they are following," Jacob cares about who he is following and on journey became deeply spiritual and vividly practical. You'll see in Chapter 4 as he takes on ten doubts and then in Chapter 8 when he guides you to KYP. The book on substance is filled with nuggets, stories, wisdom, observation, and healthy analysis. I'm over 40 years pastoring now and was impressed with this man's dedication and skill; this will be the first of plenty others. Thanks, Jacob."

—Jess Strickland, Lead Pastor, Living Hope Fellowship, Beaverton

"When reading this book, I could quickly sense that Jacob was writing out of a heart posture of care and compassion for his neighbors. Throughout the book, he is very intentional about not merely talking about ideas, but to also flesh out those ideas out with examples from his own life experiences. He does a great job utilizing sports as a metaphor to help understand one's place within a local church or within other spaces in life in general. I personally feel encouraged by Jacob in my reading of this book, as it has genuinely caused me to be reminded that I am not in this life as a lone-ranger, rather I am a full participant with others in something larger than myself. That is the challenge and reward of following the Way of Jesus."

—Hakeem Bradley, Associate Researcher Scholar, BibleProject

"A fresh, challenging, and encouraging Millennial perspective on the value and role of the believer in the local church and the Body of Christ. Author Jacob Miller writes to his readers with integrity, wisdom, and insight. He weaves together insight ranging from disciplines in sports to disappointment and rewards as they apply to the contemporary believer and the local church. He offers true spiritual insight and practical wisdom worthy of pondering and applying to a life determined to live in fruitfulness and fulfillment."

—Glenda Malmin, Professor, Portland Bible College

"A must read! This book provides believers with practical ways of finding their purpose and niche within their church body. Full of scriptural truth, Jacob does an excellent job encouraging and convicting believers to go further and step into the fullness of who God has called them to be! Prepare to be equipped!"

—Casey Benson, Professional Basketball Player

"With a voice of youth and wisdom, Jacob engages readers both young and old to consider the values of commitment to Christ, discipleship, and responsibility for the next generation. Jacob reflects on his own experiences and the profound opportunities that have been afforded to him through athletics, education, and his relentless commitment to serve the church. There is no philosophy here, just practical honest application of principles that yield results when a person is fully surrendered to the Lord Jesus Christ."

—Alex Hernandez, Lead Pastor, Lake Tahoe Christian Fellowship

"We live in a season of history when negative opinions about the Church abound. These have contributed to the large exodus of people from church attendance that has been a characteristic of the last five years. It is now important for there to be voices that call people back to the importance of the regular gathering of God's people. Jacob presents such an invitation through analogies that have worked through the years to help individuals work together with others to accomplish their united goals. It presents old ideas in a way that modern minds can comprehend them."

—Lanny Hubbard, Professor of Theology, Portland Bible College

"I appreciate Jacob's vulnerability and openness as he gives his perspective on doing church. This book provides a fresh take and practical guide to finding a church home for new believers.

—Simone Charley, Professional Soccer Player

"A fresh, honest, and youthful perspective for the local church. Jacob connects the practical with the spiritual. His extensive background in basketball gives a new understanding to the value of spiritual connection."

—Daniel Schmoll, Lead Pastor of 20+ years, Author, and Founder of Hannah House Orphanage

Finding Your Role

FINDING YOUR ROLE

How an Athletic Concept Helps Us Understand the Part that We Play in Church and in Life

JACOB MILLER

© 2022, Jacob Miller. All rights reserved.

All Scripture quotations, unless otherwise indicated, are taken from the Holy Bible, New International Version®, NIV®. Copyright ©1973, 1978, 1984, 2011 by Biblica, Inc.™ Used by permission of Zondervan. All rights reserved worldwide. **www.zondervan.com** The "NIV" and "New International Version" are trademarks registered in the United States Patent and Trademark Office by Biblica, Inc.™

Scripture quotations marked ESV are from the ESV® Bible (The Holy Bible, English Standard Version®), copyright © 2001 by Crossway Bibles, a publishing ministry of Good News Publishers. Used by permission. All rights reserved.

Scripture quotations marked (KJV) are taken from the KING JAMES VERSION, public domain.

Cover design: Caleb Keel
Cover image and interior line drawings: Rhuan Carneiro
Author photograph: Caleb Keel

Special thanks to Riley Hamilton for his gracious permission to use his photographs of the Sea of Galilee and the Dead Sea. The copyright of the images and all rights pertaining to remain the sole possession of the photographer, Riley Hamilton.

ISBN: 979-8-9853316-0-8 (paperback)
ISBN: 979-8-9853316-1-5 (ebook)

Table of Contents

Foreword
Acknowledgments
Introduction 1
Section 1: Understanding Church.. 5
    Chapter 1: Why Church? 7
    Chapter 2: What Is *Ekklesia*?.. 13
    Chapter 3: How Does *Ekklesia* Operate? 23
    Chapter 4: Kill the Doubts 29
Section 2: Playing Your Part 39
    Chapter 5: Healing from Church Hurt 41
    Chapter 6: Finding Your Home 49
    Chapter 7: Bonding With Your Team 55
    Chapter 8: KYP 61
    Chapter 9: Let It Flow 75
    Chapter 10: Who Got Next? 89
Conclusion 107
Notes 110

Foreword

As I near the fifty-year mark in my service to Portland Bible College, I find myself reflecting not so much on my own journey but rather the life outcomes of those students I have taught and mentored through the decades. In doing this I am overwhelmed with joy and gratitude in seeing how my small investments in so many lives have reaped such great rewards. With 5,000 graduates serving in over sixty nations, I now have friends all over the world. In this I have wealth beyond measure.

Jacob Miller came to PBC in the fall of 2014 and graduated in the spring of 2018 with a Bachelor of Theology including a specialization in Pastoral Ministry. It didn't take long for me to notice his hunger to learn and grow, his sincere passion for Christ, and his desire to make a difference in the lives of others. It was my privilege to watch him grow into a man of God during those years. He was not only a good student academically but, more importantly, consistently applied himself to implementing what he was learning in the youth ministry of his home church just outside of Portland. I admired his capacity to do what not very many college students do—take a full-time academic load, work a part-time job and graduate with no debt, give significant hours weekly to serving his church, and play on our college basketball team (which meant heading to practices at 5:00 a.m.). In all of this, his selfless commitment to serve came shining through.

When Jacob gave me this manuscript to read and asked if I would write this foreword, I found it easy to say yes. Though I can enjoy reading someone's theorizing, I always prefer to receive from someone who is living out what they proffer. This book represents a genuine journey of growth and discovery.

In our journey to answer life's biggest questions, perhaps one of the most helpful ones could be "Is life all about me or not?" Too often the world around us leads us, pushes us, and even beats us into an all too narcissistic approach to life. Then in the midst of this plague of self-centeredness our attempts to find community are fraught with the perils of selfishness. We struggle with how much of our commitment and involvement in community should be about our needs or those of others. It's the way of Christ that saves us from this lostness. His teachings were summed up by Paul in the phrase "It is more blessed to give than to receive" (Acts 20:35). It turns out that selfless commitment to Christ and His cause is the best way to find ourselves.

As you read this book, Jacob will take you on a journey of both understanding Christ's community, the church, and wrestling with some of the issues that make that journey both real and redemptive. In a day when many people treat churches much like restaurants, critiquing their "menu and service," Jacob makes a sound case for emulating the example of Christ. If he died for the church, maybe we should do better at living for it.

I especially identify with the use of his experience in basketball as a metaphor in the second half of this book. I grew up playing basketball, loved the game, and ended up being a volunteer high school coach for fifteen years. I found it to be a dynamic experience to teach many useful life lessons. As a coach I called it the "little game that prepares you for the big game of serving God." As a team game it has so many parallels to being a part of the church, including how to find and play your role. Dick Iverson, who founded our church and college, taught what has become a mantra to many of us: "What I'm part of is more important than the part I play."

I trust that as you follow Jacob on this journey you will be inspired and equipped to "find your role."

—Ken Malmin, Dean, Portland Bible College

Acknowledgments

This book has been quite the journey! Its conception began in 2017, while I was a senior in Bible college, and after roughly four years of slowly working on it as much the busyness of life would let me, I am so extremely excited that it is finished! I would like to take this moment to say thank you to some people who were huge impacts in my life personally and also helped in the completion of this book.

    Mom and Dad, thank you for everything you do. Dad, thank you for helping be my strength during some of my lowest moments. Thank you for supporting me throughout my life and helping me with every random thing that I might ask you about. I always knew that no matter what I may get myself into, you would be with me in it. Mom, thank you for teaching me how to love people. You've always had a big heart for others, and that was a great example for me growing up. Thank you both for keeping me in church, praying for me throughout the years, showing me how to have fun, teaching me how to be an absolute weirdo, and for your constant support throughout my athletic career. I know that I have you two in my corner whatever I do. I love you both so much!

    Pastor Daniel and Pastor Matt, thank you both for playing a part in my development as a youth pastor and a leader in the church. Thank you for giving me opportunities to lead, grace when I've failed, and wisdom when I needed it.

Ken Malmin, Glenda Malmin, Lanny Hubbard, Travis Arnold, and Carlos Marin, thank you for the four-plus years of pouring so much of your knowledge and wisdom into me while I was at PBC!

Coach Arnold, thank you for not only being my coach for four years but for playing your part in growing me as a man and looking deeper into your players than just their basketball skills.

Caleb Keel, thank you for continually having a heart to serve people. Also, thank you for helping design this amazing cover for this book.

The Boyer family, thank you for being my second family! Alice and Doug, you two gave me a model of what a godly marriage and family looks like. Josh, thank you for taking me under your wing and really mentoring me when I needed a big brother in my life the most! Thank you all for letting me into your home when I was a goober child and sharing your family with me. I will never forget your example!

My VSM Family—a very special thank you to all of my Viral Student Ministries family. Being your youth pastor the past four years has been one of the greatest blessings in my life. It is an absolute honor that God would trust me with leading an amazing group of students like you all. Getting to watch you all grow in your relationships with Jesus is something that I will never forget. The most exciting part now is for me to see you all get older and apply the things that you learned in youth group to the rest of your lives. God has an amazing plan for each one of you, and I hope this book will help guide you in your path toward Jesus. Many things in this book are things I wish I had been told when I was your age, so I hope you take notes. Because note takers are …

Introduction

There is no doubt that if you begin to pause your church normalcy and look at yourself and the rest of the congregation, you will discover an underlying issue. Some people will speak to it, some will hide it, but all the while most do not even know that it exists. The reality is that there is a serious case of Christians feeling detached, dispassionate, or maybe never even feeling a part of their church.

    I grew up in a small town outside Portland, Oregon, called Scappoose, and in the Pacific Northwest, there are more churches than you might think. However, I look around at the surrounding churches, both small and large, and I can see the same problem. Some churches do a better job while others struggle more, but few have mastered this art of creating a place for *all* who believe that Jesus is their Lord and Savior. The whole topic of church is a weird, interesting, and increasingly more debated topic. Why, though? Doesn't Jesus call us to come together in community? So why are people not wanting to come under one building to have *ekklesia* together?

    Well, I think that a large part of that is because Christians have a hard time finding their place in the church. Although I believe that the church has a role to play in finding a place for all believers, I will be speaking directly to you. The church member, the regular churchgoer, the occasional church attendee, the only-on-holidays church congregant—you!

I do not think your spiritual walk is contingent on whether you feel welcome at church or not. Your spiritual walk with Christ is in *your own hands*, and I believe it is time you take ownership of that!

Someone once said, "The church is not for you. But it is for the world!" What does that even mean? And how can you say that the church is not for me? Well, throughout this book, I will break down and discuss the multitudes of reasons why believers can find themselves in this funk and how I believe that the athletic world can actually shed some light to how we (as Christians) can find our role in this whole confusing thing that we call church and life.

I played basketball my entire life, all the way, even through college. And even as I write this now, as a graduate from college, I still play basketball for adult leagues because I cannot get away from the game. Growing up, I played all kinds of sports, both team sports and more individual ones, such as track and field. In sports, you realize that you are part of something larger than yourself. In sports, you realize that you cannot do everything, let alone do them all well. In sports, you are taught what it looks like to work as a team to achieve a common goal.

Regardless of whether you have never touched a ball in your life or played three sports all the way through college, I want to encourage you to be open to hearing something new. In basketball, there are many different roles that people are in, such as the coach, the star player, the starters, the role-players, the water boy or girl, the team manager, etc. The issue can be that some of those people can idolize the star player, thinking that they don't have as much value as that player. But that's absolutely not true.

Every person has a role to play on every team, and your role can look different on every team you're on. Every person in every role has an equal effect on the success of the team, and your role does not define your value. I'm confident that understanding this model of athletics can help you find your role in this life of a believer and your role in the church. So if you are at a point in your life where you feel lost, uncertain, and unsure what your role is in the church, or even what your role is in this life as a follower of Christ, then please keep reading, because it is my goal to help you determine your role.

I believe in what the Bible says in Proverbs 29:18: "Where there is no vision, the people perish" (KJV). I also look at the Israelites and their history of wandering and wandering and wandering. This is my motive and heart behind this book. If I can help God's people from losing vision and wandering, then I will do it. That is my prayer and hope in this book—that it will help guide you and keep you on the path to which God has called you. So throughout this book, I will be laying out a chapter-by-chapter, step-by-step process to lead us all to a mutual understanding and conclusion at the end, where my hope is that we will all be better equipped for this journey.

SECTION 1: UNDERSTANDING CHURCH

Chapter 1: Why Church?

The society into which the Christian is called at baptism is not a collective but a Body.

—C. S. Lewis

This seems to be the biggest issue for the generations at hand, so this is how we are going to spearhead this book: Why church? Why go to a church building? Why sing songs? Why have a message or sermon? Why take communion? Why do we do all these religious things?

Why?

Before I dive too deep into this topic, I do want to say that I will not be addressing every benefit of the church and every "why" for needing it. As much as I would love to, I don't think either of us has enough time to read the expansiveness that would be, so I will attempt to relay the mere necessities of why church.

There is a hard pushback on the idea of church being a communal thing that meets in a building because of the movement of *"We* are the church." This belief is actually not that ridiculous considering that the apostle Paul had greeted the congregation of believers (church) that would meet in Priscilla and Aquila's house.

> Greet Priscilla and Aquila my helpers in Christ Jesus: Who have for my life laid down their own necks: unto whom not only I give thanks, but also all the churches of the Gentiles. Likewise greet

the church that is in their house. Salute my well-beloved Epaenetus, who is the firstfruits of Achaia unto Christ. (Romans 16:3–5)

Notice how Paul did not greet the house that they would meet in, rather the living and breathing people who met inside it. First off, it would be very odd if Paul was talking and greeting an inanimate object, though never put it past God to incline someone. But that was never the intention of the Scriptures. The church was and always has been more than the place where you meet.

But can I warn you? Do not go too far into the other end of the spectrum, the end that says, "There is no point in going to church on Sundays because I read the Bible, pray, etc." The danger of this extreme is all too real when you consider the fact that church is a sacred place where the believers build one another up, edify each other, and glorify God!

This entire topic has got so interesting as I have been writing this book. During my time of writing this, we have endured the COVID-19 pandemic, which completely rocked the foundation of churches worldwide! At least from my hometown here, we had to do online-only church services. It was horrible! Wait, but Jacob, aren't you a youth pastor and on staff at your church? How could you say that it was horrible? Weren't you the same person who was saying, "I'm so *pumped* for online service this week"?

Yup.

But let me tell you ... it was a struggle!

You really don't realize how much you miss something until you have it stripped away, and that is exactly what COVID-19 did to churches worldwide. Suddenly, we couldn't see our friends at church, grab post-church lunch with people, hug one another, lay hands and pray for our church family, and the worst one—we couldn't worship together!!!

I missed it *so* much after about three weeks. And honestly, the hardest part was that we would have to meet via livestreams, Zoom calls, and such. We interacted digitally and solely digitally. Thank you, Jesus, for technology, but it does not substitute for the real deal. It was like a tease. I could see people in these video group chats, watch our worship team (two people at least) worship on a Sunday YouTube video, and listen to our pastor bring a word with two people in the entire sanctuary that can seat more than two hundred people. But I couldn't be there. It was making the best of what we had at the time, but *it was not church*! As much as we could try to make it normal, it was not normal because when you take the *people* away from one another, there is a longing to be in community once again.

I missed the people. The corporate worship. The prayer. The atmosphere. The anointing. The greeters. The ushers. The realness! I missed church! That season of not being able to meet physically truly taught me that I simply cannot handle being away from church and my people!

Relationship versus Religion

I often hear the argument of "relationship is greater than religion" when in talks with people who disagree with the weekly meetings of churches. For some reason, there is just a draw to go away from any type of religion and pull toward the relationship side of Christianity, and that *alone*.

I fully agree that the largest difference between Christianity and any other religion is the fact that we are not the ones who are first going after God, but rather God first went after us—the fact that we do indeed have a relationship with our Savior! He is not some far and distant God who watches the chaos of the world on his big-screen TV. No, He is a very involved God who loves to be with His children! This is our biggest difference maker when comparing YHWH to any other God and religion. Should we embrace that? Absolutely. That is why we have the light; that is why we are saved; that is why we have a relationship with God!

But ...

Let's not forget that we in fact have some religiosity about our belief system:

- We believe in the power of water baptism.
- We believe in partaking in the table of the Lord (Communion).

- We believe that we must surrender our lives daily and let sanctification do its work that we may be in right relationship with the Father (sanctification).

Those sound pretty religious, don't they?

People often will turn away from things they are uncertain about or things that bring about discomfort. If you don't understand water baptism, then it will seem dumb and pointless to you. If you don't understand the table of the Lord, then you think it is some washed-out ritual. And if you don't understand sanctification, then it seems like some kind of religious rite of passage. Discomfort is a huge turnoff for many new Christians or "pre-believers." Because who wants to feel uncomfortable?

The reality is that Christ actually called us into a life of being uncomfortable. Yay! I know how excited you are to hear that. As upsetting as that may be for some people, that is the truth of what Christ expects of us. Let me encourage you with a passage from John:

> If the world hates you, know that it has hated me before hating you. If you were of the world, the world would love you as its own; but because you are not of the world, but I chose you out of this world, therefore the world hates you. (John 15:18–29 ESV)

If that wasn't encouraging enough, check out what Jesus says in Matthew 10:22: "And you will be hated by all for my name's sake. But the one who endures to the end will be saved" (ESV). I don't know about you, but I feel super motivated to go out to make an impact for the kingdom of God after reading that stuff! All jokes aside, Christ says some amazing things in those passages that we need to pay attention to in order to catch what He is saying. In the passage from Matthew, He concludes by saying that the one who endures will be saved. What does that even mean? Well to me, it means that this journey is not a sprint but rather it is a marathon. Which means that I need to understand that this journey may have some moments where things will hinge on my comfort or discomfort.

Our modern day reality is that people care more about their following than *who* they are following. You see this more often in the Millenials and Gen Z generations. You have social media and you see who follows you. But do you ever question *why* they are following you? Do you ever think about what they are receiving from you? The content? The message you send? The morals you portray?

Maybe this is part of the reason why many people have a hard time getting engaged and connected to a church. The fact that many could say, *I believe most of what they say or teach, but not all of it!* This can actually be a real hindrance to many people because they are looking for that perfect, hand-in-glove kind of fit.

But if that is how you think, can I challenge you with a thought? Very seldom do you ever find a church that believes *everything* the same way you do. Obviously the core beliefs and basic doctrine and theology need to line up, but what about the negotiables—the things that in comparison to salvation and knowing Jesus, don't really matter?

"But I don't believe in raising my hands in worship!"

"But I don't like how they have two senior pastors!"

"But I don't like how they don't have a ministry for young adults!"

When you always find something to disagree with, I question whether or not you ever *do* want to agree with anything. Regardless of what you believe with those little things, there are core beliefs that must fall in line with the Scriptures: That Jesus is the Lord and Savior, and that He was fully man and fully God. That He lived a perfect and spotless life, died on the cross, rose on the third day and defeated death, and before ascending to heaven to be with the Father, He sent humankind His Holy Spirit to be our Advocate!

Boom!

Do you agree with that? Okay, then we are on the same team here.

We can spend all our time going back and forth with theories on why people don't like or want to go to church, but that isn't the point of this chapter. My aim is to help you understand that we need to humble ourselves and surrender what we think to the truth and Word of God. Let the Word of God change our thoughts and beliefs rather than letting our thoughts and beliefs change what the Word of God says. *And His Word calls for His people to be together.*

There is no way around it. It is as simple as this: If Jesus is our model for everything, as He should be, then let's look at Him for this. Jesus surrounded Himself with people of like-mindedness, didn't He? One could even say that He had His own little church. He had His disciples with Him in community, and that is our model! If that isn't enough to convince you that community is vastly important, just look at the God that we serve: We believe in the Trinity, that God is One but Three—the Father, the Son, and the Holy Spirit.

Even God lives in community! So there is our model. That is enough to tell us why we need church so badly!

Chapter 2: What Is *Ekklesia*?

> Unity is necessary to the outpouring of the Spirit of God. If you have 120 volts of electricity coming into your house but you have broken wiring, you may turn on the switch, but nothing works—no lights come on, the stove doesn't warm, the radio doesn't turn on. Why? Because you have broken wiring. The power is ready to do its work ..., but where there is broken wiring, there is no power. Unity is necessary among the children of God if we are going to know the flow of power... to see God do His wonders. (A. W. Tozer)[1]

I assume that most of you have never been to Bible college or seminary, so I am going to try to give you some Bible college study as briefly and summarized as much as possible. This word may not mean anything to you *yet*, but it will!

Ekklesia

What in the world is that?

Ekklesia is the Greek word that we get church from. It is found in the New Testament 114 times, and of those 114 times, the word is used in four different ways:

- It represents the body of Christ *worldwide*, over which the Lord functions as head (Matthew 16:18; Ephesians 1:22; 1 Timothy 3:15).
- The expression can refer to God's people in a given *region* (Acts 9:31).
- Frequently, it depicted a *local congregation* of Christians (1 Corinthians 1:2; Revelation 1:11).[2]
- It could also signify a group of the Lord's people *assembled* for worship (1 Corinthians 14:34–35).

But according to the *NIV Exhaustive Concordance*, the actual definition of *ekklesia* is:

> ***ekklesia*** [114]—church, congregation, assembly; a group of people gathered together. It can refer to the OT assembly of believers (Ac. 7:38), or a riotous mob (Ac. 19:32), but usually to a Christian assembly, a church; as totality (Eph. 3:10), or in a specific locale (Col. 4:15). In the NT a church is never a building or meeting place: church (74), churches (34), assembly (4), congregation (1), congregations (1).[3]

There is another word, though, that refers to us as the church. This word is *koinonia*, another Greek word, and by definition (b), it means:

> ***koinonia*** [19]- Fellowship, the close association between persons, emphasizing what is common between them; by extension: participation, sharing, contribution, gift, the outcome of such close relationships:- fellowship (10), sharing (3), participation (2), contribution (1), fellowship of sharing (1), partnership (1), share (1).[4]

Koinonia in the Twenty-First Century

In 2010, when I was fifteen years old, I endured one of the hardest seasons of my life. In general, life never has too many consistencies, but when I was growing up, I had one thing that I could always count on—my family. My parents raised me in the church and raised me up with not only good morals and values but also a faith in Jesus, and I am forever grateful for that! Growing up, I had many friends say to me that my family (meaning my parents) were the definition of a perfect family. We went to church, loved Jesus, had fun, laughed, and all those good things. My sister and brother are much older, so I was basically an only child at that point. I had a security in my mind that I may not have this or that, but at least I have the *best* family and parents.

Now fast-forward to my freshman year of high school, and I found my parents on the threshold of divorce and myself completely alone. I had *nobody* to turn to—nobody I felt I could trust, nobody I felt I could get close to, nobody I could vent to and confide in. This was the defining moment in my walk with Jesus because it was in this moment when my life and everything I had trusted and never questioned crumbled to the ground and flipped upside down. There was a night when I was completely broken, tears in my eyes, with no idea what to do. I sprinted up to my room to grab my Bible, which I had never truly read. I hugged that thing ever so tightly and cried out to God, saying "Lord, I have *nothing*! All I have is you, and I need you, Lord!"

Along with this, I made a promise to God that I would start consistently attending church, which I had been irregular in to say the least. Coincidentally, the next day after this defining moment in my faith was Wednesday, which was youth group night at my church. It was completely dark out as I walked up to the church building. I went by myself and honestly knew nobody that went, either. It had been a couple years since I went last (I had only gone a handful of times), and I was on the verge of a breakdown as it was. My life had gone into chaos in a matter of days, and no one knew about it yet. So I opened the door and walked in.

I didn't see anyone at first until I turned the first corner in the hallway, and there was my youth pastor. I couldn't believe it, but he actually remembered my name! He said, "Hey Jacob! What's up, man? How are you doing?"

Without even saying two full words, I utterly broke down. I tried containing myself, but I just started to tear up, and I couldn't say a word without it getting worse. He obviously could tell something was up, so he said to come into the office real quick. He asked me what was going on, but again I couldn't get any words out. I was too much of a mess to make any sense, so he just responded by praying for me, and then we went out. Now I was red-eyed and not able to talk to anyone, not that it really mattered because I didn't know anyone when I walked into the sanctuary anyway.

And then it happened.

The emcee went up to start service and we started worship. And the floodgates of heaven opened as well as the floodgates of my eyes. I just wept and wept and wept. God met with me there, and from this one moment, I began to get connected with people and leaders in the youth group.

I started to feel that this place was actually my home, and these people were my family. I had never felt that before, at least not at church (maybe that's why I was so inconsistent in my church attendance). I started to have real connections with the youth pastor, youth leaders, and other youth students! I felt more at home with them than I did at my own home.

What started to happen and what made everything different for me was that I was beginning to understand and feel *koinonia* firsthand!

What Have We Become?

If you have looked into the news at any point in the last couple decades (especially more recently), you would have to be pretty naive to think that there is nothing happening in our world that should cause us to feel concerned. Regardless of your thoughts and political views, if you tune into a news station, you see mass shootings, police brutality, children being murdered in the womb, immorality being embraced with open arms, local governments endorsing addiction in the name of making an income, and more. If you did some research on what is happening in our *world* and not just our *country*, it is even worse and more blatant! People are getting targeted and killed for their faith, corrupt governments are attacking their own people or just simply not protecting their people, which results in severe oppression against women and girls, civil war, drug cartels having more power than local governments, and more!

I am in my twenties as I write this, and as more and more of these things became normal in our society as a whole, I have heard many, many times people in the church say, *It's the end times!* or *Jesus is coming! Blah, blah, blah!*

Remember the hysteria at the beginning of the COVID-19 pandemic? Remember every single old-aged Christian that you knew who said, "Jesus is coming back! It's soon!" Yeah, me too!

I'm sorry, I don't mean to come off condescending here, but I don't exactly care so much about that stuff! I just don't! We have been in the end times for a very long time now! In fact, we have technically been in the "end of days" since Jesus was resurrected. I *know* Jesus is coming soon! And we have known that He is for a long time!

I know that it is important to understand the season that you are in, but what I care about more than that, is *acting in the season that you are in*!

When I was growing up, my dad was always in the business world, and something that he would often say to me as I continued to aspire to go into the corporate business world myself, is this: "Anyone can point out a problem or issue, but a *leader* is someone who has a solution to it."

I feel like the church has kind of got this negative reputation and now we are trying to backtrack.

We have somewhat taken ownership of this role of being a whistleblower. At least in the last few decades, the church has become this sort of loudmouth in our society, and the world hasn't taken too kindly to that. It truly breaks my heart when I drive around Portland and see people holding up signs that say, "God hates gays!" and "Gays are going to burn in hell!"

I mean, *Wow!* Where has our compassion and love for people gone?

When I hear the awful things that the church and self-proclaimed Christians have said about the LGBTQ community and others, I can understand why people don't want to come to church. I mean, they must think, *Why would I want to know Jesus if these people who claim to be His followers are driven with hate for me?*

When you start to hate sin more than you love people, you begin to follow the footsteps of the Pharisees, and what did Jesus say about them? Sometimes we allow ourselves to sacrifice *compassion* in the name of *truth*.

I have been saying this since my freshman year of Bible college, but the church as a whole has taken on this role of yelling at sin and condemning people instead of loving people. We have been pushing people further and further away from Jesus, and we are responsible ourselves for much of the terrible reputation that the church has in the twenty-first century. I am sorry to say that, and I know it hurts. In fact, it *should* hurt. We have been doing the opposite of our calling to bring in disciples because we are condemning the very people Jesus died to save!

Now please do not hear what I am not saying, because I am in *no* way condoning sin and our sinful world. Yes, I believe that our world is "going to hell in a handbasket" and our world is going further and further away from God. We are indeed in a post-Christian society. I do agree with all those things, but what I disagree with is *how* we are being followers of Christ to those around us!

I heard it best at a Foursquare Church leadership conference when the speaker said, "Hold onto truth and do not forfeit truth, but you front with love!" What he was saying is that we do not approve the sin, but we front like Jesus did and love them first!

After all, love is one of the things that separated Jesus from the Pharisees. The people had tradition, law, reputation, religion, and then all of a sudden, this so-called "messiah" guy comes on the scene and has compassion for people who "weren't supposed to be loved"—homeless people, people sick of leprosy, disabled people, social outcasts, people viewed as less than," etc. Jesus is our master role model, and if that is true, what do we read in 1 John 4:8? "Whoever does not love does not know God, because God is love."

It doesn't just say that God has love, or that He gives love. It says that He *is* love! God is the epitome of what love is. We have corrupted what that word means, but I am not going into that because that could be a whole sermon right there. To put it briefly, the God kind of love is one that is pure and cares for people. Look at the Gospels and see how many times Jesus was "moved with compassion" for people. It never said that Jesus was disgusted with these sinful people and yelled at them and their sin, and then walked away.

Jesus was fully man but also fully God, right? You have to believe that as Jesus would walk around and people would brush shoulders with Him, He already knew all of their secret struggles, issues, and sin. Yet He still had compassion for them—so much so that He lived a perfect and sinless life, endured a horrendous and morbid death, and then resurrected on the third day to defeat sin and death entirely forever!

That's a good place to say amen!

There it is. Jesus died to give people, who don't deserve righteousness, a chance to come into relationship with the Father. That's amazing! And that's the gospel!

That is how we ought to be. I could know all the dirt on somebody (and some people are more open about their dirt), but it is my *mission* to love them regardless and do my very best to represent Jesus well and invite them into a relationship with Him. After all, I don't care who you are and how good of a person you are, you and I do not deserve salvation or righteousness, yet we receive it in faith through Christ. Thank you, Jesus, for grace.

So with the craziness and ungodliness that is in our world, my question remains this: What is the church doing about it?

Are we yelling at the problem (sin)? Or are we bringing the solution—Jesus?

Family Is Key

Unfortunately our reputation as a church and body of Christ has been soiled, and the one who is most to blame is ourselves. But there is hope!

I'm beginning to see much of the worldwide church has begun to see our flaws in this, and many people and local churches are trying to reconcile what has been done and said. This is good. But for most worldly people, it is not enough. So here is where many Christians start to go down the extreme path of "relationship is greater than religion."

They will blame religion for all the hate and pain that the church has caused. They will use the Pharisees as an example, and they will endorse that the answer is not religion but rather, a *relationship* with Jesus. And they are completely right. But there is a balance here. The temptation is to go too deep into the extreme of actually rebuking religion, and that is harmful to our faith.

Wherever you fall on this scale, you cannot deny that we need a relationship with Jesus. That is what makes us different from other beliefs. We believe that through Jesus Christ, we in fact have a personal relationship with God. But you also cannot deny that we are also religious. Like I said earlier in the book, we do many sacraments and rituals, and Jesus endorsed them Himself.

So my answer to this fight is this: The answer is not to kill out religion with relationship; instead it is to redefine what religion is!

The largest reason I got so connected and invested in my church and youth group while going through my parents' divorce was because it was a family. I got so deeply connected with multiple people in the youth group, where I had many moments when I could be vulnerable and heal from my trauma. It was a safe place for me to let God work on my heart and heal my innermost being. A family focus is so important for us to remember because Satan will throw so many lies at us, trying to separate us from our intimacy with our church family because he knows the power in family.

When I look at all the problems and issues in our country, my first thought is, *How different would all of this look if we had strong families*?

Look at our culture in the United States of America. How many divorces do you see? How many absent parents do children have? How many fathers are gone and not raising their kids? How many single mothers are having to work three jobs to pay for their children's food & clothes because Dad isn't there to help? How common is it to have kids outside of the confines of marriage?

Let's see some statistics on divorce:

- As of 2018, in the U.S.A. there is one divorce every thirteen seconds.
- Almost half of all marriages will end in divorce.
- Researchers estimate that 41% of first marriages will end in divorce.
- 60% of second marriages will end in divorce.
- 73% of third marriages will end in divorce. [5]

And as of 2017, children younger than 18:
- 21% live with a solo mother.
- 4% live with solo father.
- 7% live with cohabiting mother and father.
- 65% live with married parents.[6]

So why do so many young people have all these bad thoughts, problems, etc.? Why do they support such ungodly things in our culture? Why is the Millennial generation the prime scapegoat for issues in our society? Some allegations are in fact true, but ... *why?* Could it be because these people had absent parents and thus had no one to raise them? I also want to note that just because you are physically present in your marriage and the raising of your children, it doesn't make you mentally, emotionally, and spiritually present.

I believe that the Enemy has had a foothold on our culture in the United States of America and has attacked family values in the twenty-first century because having family is godly. Jesus died on a tree in order to bring us into His family. He calls for His church to be a family. We are to have fellowship and to be brothers and sisters in Christ!

If we are to walk in the power that Christ died to give us, then we need to embrace family as a church.

Chapter 3: How Does *Ekklesia* Operate?

I want the whole Christ for my Saviour, the whole Bible for my book, the whole Church for my fellowship, and the whole world for my mission field.

—John Wesley

I will always admit that I am prone to being an overly practical person. I just figure that having good knowledge, facts, and wisdom are great and all, but it is pointless if you don't know how to incorporate it and use it for something.

So …

How is the church supposed to operate? What is the actual function of the church?

Our modern take of church is very event-inspired. If you went to a church and they showed you their church calendar, you would find that churches plan many, many, many events every year! Outreach events, missions fundraising, special holiday services, youth parties, small group outings, etc. Churches plan events after events and if you are involved in your church planning team, then you know that it can often feel like once you are done with one event, you move on to planning the next one. It never stops. You can even look at most churches on a Sunday service—the stage lights, the signs, the screens, the cool moving backgrounds, the computers, the awkward clicks from the photographer capturing the service, the booming sound system, the stage fog, etc. is meant to make it feel like an event.

So a question must be raised ... Is the function of the church supposed to be like this? Is this how we ought to operate?

Well, as with all things, we should look to Scripture and find our answers.

What's Our Mission Here?

The mission and focus of the church should include the following:

1. Make disciples (Matthew 28:19–20).

The last thing that Jesus told the disciples in the gospel of Matthew is "Therefore go and make disciples of all nations, baptizing them in the name of the Father and of the Son and of the Holy Spirit, and teaching them to obey everything I have commanded you" (Matthew 28:19–20). I am personally, very passionate about discipleship!

Discipleship is an area the church can do better in, and I want to help in the progress of it. Discipleship is often neglected due to our Western church culture that tells us to simply get people to the "door of salvation" and then move on to the next person. I can't read the New Testament and think this is the best way for making disciples. I've seen too many people come to say the sinner's prayer and then get left behind in the nuances of church. They have questions and struggles, and sin that still plagues them, but they are left alone spiritually to figure it all out on their own.

I say this to church leaders and future church leaders: Can we please not abandon our brothers in sisters in Christ when they are infants in the faith? Just as you wouldn't leave a five-year-old child to figure out how to live the rest of their life by themselves, we shouldn't do that with people in their faith walk either.

2. Preach the gospel of Jesus (2 Timothy 4:2).

"Preach the word; ... correct, rebuke and encourage—with great patience and careful instruction"

Say that! Preach it, preacher. Amen. The church must be preaching the good news of Jesus Christ! This one is may be seen more than the others because most churches do preach about Jesus. However, just to provoke some deeper thought and conversation here, when was the last time that you heard your pastor actually preach a sermon or teach on the saving power of the gospel of Jesus? Like truly think about it ... preaching the gospel of Jesus doesn't mean that you cannot preach out of the other books in the Bible not named Matthew, Mark, Luke, and John. However, you must be able to tie in the sermon to the good news of the gospel of Jesus!

3. Show the world the love of Jesus (1 John 4:19–20).

Arguably the most challenging aspect of being a Christian is showing the world around us the genuine and unconditional love of Jesus—withholding our own biases and prejudices toward people we don't like or agree with, and still loving these people in a Christlike, servitude type of way. When done correctly, it's beautiful. When done correctly, the church stands completely out when compared to the secular world of today.

The question that many theologians have argued back and forth on—Is it about the action of loving or about preaching the truth?—is not valid, because it is both. Not one or the other, but rather it's both. It's a paradox of thinking that will cause many to struggle with their own personal convictions, but through the Holy Spirit, it can be done! Preaching the truth while loving people in the process.

4. Show unity among all believers (1 Corinthians 12:12; Philippians 2:1–4).

God makes a specific call and command for His children to be unified under the name of Jesus. No ifs, buts, or ands but rather a simple *"Okay, I will"* can suffice for our response to this command. Our God is a God of unity and seeks for His people to represent that here on earth. After all, we are supposed to be the representation of Jesus among the people and world that we live in. And what I see in the Scriptures is that God Himself lives in unity—the Father, Son, and Holy Spirit, in perfect unity! If God lives in unity, I suppose we ought to as well.

A Shift Is Happening

Just the other day, I was having a great conversation with one of my cousins about how the various levels of church size really impact the feel of being a part of a church. Something that he said struck me. "I have a hard time with big churches because you can go there on a Sunday and maybe talk to a couple people and leave without making any real or lasting connections. It doesn't feel like family," he said.

I could argue with him on that. However, it is without a doubt difficult to make true relationships with the church leadership especially. The college that I went to was associated with a very large church, and I still joke with one of my ministry friends because I had "met" him about seventeen times before he finally remembered who I was.

Although this is hilarious, and I still joke about it today, it wasn't his fault. It is hard to meet and talk to nearly a hundred people weekly and then try to remember the faces and names the next time you may see them. That is tough. And if you have some sort of bitterness because you were offended by a pastor for not remembering you, I would be interested to see how you would do in a minister's shoes like theirs.

After my cousin had made this statement, I told him, "I completely agree with you about that. But the thing is that our modern local churches are beginning to shift." What is happening is that churches are shifting their focus, less on Sunday morning and evening services and more on small groups.

How can a church that meets in a ministadium with over 1,000 people attending be a family? Well, do they have small groups available? Because this is where family is built. I know that in my parents' generation, Sunday mornings were the pinnacle of church. They were all about meeting, gathering, being family, and all this good stuff. But most of these churches lacked in size that would warrant small groups being formed. Many larger churches *must* have small groups. Otherwise, they become an event, not a church!

HOW DOES *EKKLESIA* OPERATE?

Small groups do many things, but some of the most important of these include accountability, responsibility, integrity, *ekklesia*, and intimacy with fellow believers.

If you are currently attending a large church and feel disconnected there, please find someone, and ask them if they know about how to get involved with a small group in the church. I promise that they likely have them, and that might just cure your frustration!

Chapter 4: Kill the Doubts

> When the New Testament talks about doubt, whether you're talking about the Gospels or the epistles, it primarily focuses on believers. That's very important. It's as if you have to believe something before you can doubt it; you have to be committed to it before you begin to question it. So doubt is held up as the unique problem of the believer.[7]
>
> —John MacArthur

This is where the rubber meets the road. All the information that I shared with you prior is all pointless if we haven't discussed the doubts you have toward church.

A personal struggle I have is that I can tend to be a skeptic with certain things. I always say it is a good thing to have a healthy balance of doubt, but that can potentially be very harmful in terms of the kingdom of God. When you idolize doubt, you often will resist acting in faith; thus, carrying doubt limits the move of God and inevitably moves you outside of the place that God wants you to be in.

Don't feel horrible or condemned if you have doubts about church or even God, because you are not the "worst person" and you are not even alone there. Most people, including myself, have had countless times when we have struggled with doubt about all this. But, how can someone have a healthy marriage if you are constantly thinking that your significant other is going to cheat on you? You cannot!

So it is time to kill the doubt that may be lingering in you about church. Let's cut down some common lies of the Enemy real quick and speak over it what the Word of God says.

Doubt #1: What If I Don't Desire to Pray, Worship, or Read the Bible?

Believe it or not, this is actually a very common thing for Christians, even the leaders that you see on the big screen and leaders that you see in the church. I would actually be lying if I said this isn't me sometimes. As Martyn Lloyd-Jones puts it, "Everything we do in Christian life is easier than prayer.[8]

But why? Shouldn't we always want to talk to our Creator? What is wrong with me? Maybe this is just a sign that this isn't the life that I'm supposed to live. Clearly I am not meant to be a Christian if I can't even enjoy or desire doing the things that I am supposed to do—

Nope! That is wrong. This is a struggle that every single Christian has battled with at some point, and some will always. The way that I see it is like this: If it were always fun, enjoyable, and I always got something from praying, worshipping, and reading my Bible, then where is the obedience? Let me rephrase this: If that were the case, then I would be doing those things for what it did and gave me! I wouldn't be doing it for anything else, much less out of obedience and devotion to God.

Obviously prayer, worship, and Bible reading is multifaceted, but here is how I look at it: I pray to speak to God and present my heart and hear from His heart. I worship Him because I am proclaiming that He alone is worthy to be praised. I read the Bible to learn more about His character, His heart, and why I need Him. I want you to know that although we do receive from praying, worshipping, and reading the Scriptures, what we receive should not always be our motivating factor to do these things.

Doubt #2: What Should I Do Now that I Am a Christian?

Oh boy, this is quite the loaded question, isn't it? However, this is honestly a question that every believer should have the answer to; otherwise, how else will we be great evangelists? So you have decided to follow Jesus and have declared Him as your personal Lord and Savior. Awesome!

Now what? One word: discipleship.

First, surround yourself with a community of fellow believers (a church). The reason you do this is because it is important to find people who will encourage, push you, keep you accountable, and bless you into a deeper relationship with Jesus. A godly community is irreplaceable. If the community is done right, you can't help but to grow in your relationship with God.

Second, dive into the Scriptures (Bible). If you don't know what to read and don't feel like simply googling it, don't worry. I got you. Read the gospels of Jesus. Start with Matthew, Mark, Luke, and then John. After that, connect with a Christian you know and ask them to do a Bible study with you through the book of Romans.

Many people grab the Bible and treat it like a normal book; they start reading at the beginning. However, I don't personally recommend that. I know, I know, what kind of somewhat educated person tells you to start a book halfway through? But in order to understand the rest of the Bible, you need to know about Jesus and His life first and foremost. The whole Bible will make more sense when you understand that all of it relates to Jesus Christ. And that's it! I wouldn't recommend doing anything else at this point. Just those two things.

I think we often overcomplicate things in the church, especially when talking about becoming a Christian. We expect perfection from people once they decide to follow Jesus, but that's not logical. Stop living in whatever sin you are indulging in because it will harm you in your connection to Jesus. It may not happen overnight, but it's all about progress leads to perfection.

Doubt #3: What If I Am Discouraged in Evangelizing?

That is totally fine. I think that this is actually a case-by-case situation. If you are feeling discouraged with sharing Jesus with other people, whether it be family, friends, or strangers, you need to ask yourself this one question: *Why* do I not want to share Jesus with others?

Be honest with yourself and answer this truthfully. If you do not want to share Jesus with others because you don't quite feel confident in your knowledge of God yourself, then there is your answer. Keep learning about God and grow in your relationship with Him. But if your answer is simply because you are nervous and scared of talking about it with others, then I would like to lovingly encourage you to *get over it and be okay with being uncomfortable*. Ask God to strengthen you and take a step of faith and watch how He will use you.

This may be convicting but it needs to be on all Christians' minds. If your comfort comes in the way of bringing people to Jesus, that is possibly the most selfish thing you could do. And trust me, I am guilty of this myself. Understand that our world is going further and further from God. The only thing that can save people is Jesus Christ! And we are talking eternity, not just our mortal lives here on earth. If the thing that is preventing you from possibly saving people's souls is your being uncomfortable, then you need to reevaluate your heart.

Doubt #4: How Can I Love Church Members with Different Political Views?

This is the question of our time! How in the world am I supposed to love other people that I don't even know, let alone people that I do not agree with? Can we be honest, open, and transparent a little bit?

The times that we are living in right now are some of the most politically toxic and divisive that our nation has ever seen. I am truly not exaggerating here, and you know that. Political divisiveness is not a fake thing, but rather it is something that is our reality. So we need to answer this. *How can I love someone in this church that votes Republican? How can I love someone that votes Democrat? How can they be for that!? How can they be for them!* Let us stop, take a chill pill, and read what Scripture says.

> Have nothing to do with foolish, ignorant controversies; you know that they breed quarrels. And the Lord's servant must not be quarrelsome but kind to everyone, able to teach, patiently enduring evil, correcting his opponents with gentleness. God may perhaps grant them repentance leading to a knowledge of the truth, and they may come to their senses and escape from the snare of the devil, after being captured by him to do his will.
> (2 Timothy 2:23–26 ESV)

This is powerful because to really understand this passage, you need to understand that Paul was writing this while he was literally in a dark, damp, and smelly prison cell! This man was in a prison cell and knew that his death was coming, so he wrote to prepare Timothy for his coming ministry struggles.

So why does this apply to us in this topic? Well, because it is almost as if God is speaking to us today with our political divisions in our churches, and he is saying that we need to let some things go.

Let go of the conspiracies.
Let go of the pettiness.
Let go of your grudges.
Let go of unforgiveness.
Let go of division.
Let go of your anger toward people.
Let go of controversies.
Let. It. Go.

Please don't hear what I am not saying on this, because I do not want to downplay voting, politics, and government. I believe that it is truly important to vote and for Christians to pray for our national leaders, as well as to pay attention to what is happening in government. But as far as I am concerned, I care more about bringing unity to the body of Christ, than I do about what divides the children of God from one another. There will always be things that can divide us, but thankfully, we are all bought by the same precious blood of Jesus Christ. And that right there doesn't care about who you voted for!

Doubt #5: Does Going to Church Really Matter to God?

Absolutely it does. Jesus told Peter, "On this rock, I will build my church!" Jesus is pretty focused on preparing his bride, waiting for the day that He will return to her. That is some deep stuff, but I feel pretty passionately that we need to be a part of the body of Christ if we are supposed to understand the fullness of the heart of God. God loves community. Our example is God the Father, God the Son, and God the Spirit, all coming together in unity. Perfect unity! So if we are wanting to understand God in a fuller way, then we ourselves need to be in community with fellow believers.

Doubt #6: Aren't All Religions Basically the Same?

As much as many people would love to say, *Heck, no, they aren't*, I could see how many people would also say that, from their perspective, most religions are basically the same. To be clear, I do *not* believe that all religions are the same (certainly Christianity is very different).

However, this is a growing movement. I literally just heard about how Steve Harvey calls himself a Christian, but he believes that all religions will lead to heaven. We have a very real situation of people feeling something different but not knowing why. So, let's talk about *why* Christianity is in fact different.

Christianity is the *only* religion where humanity did not go after God, but God went after humanity.

Christianity is the *only* religion where we can have an actual real relationship with God.

Christianity teaches that God forgives those who have sinned even before they have repaid their wrongs.

Christianity teaches good works *after* grace, but other religions teach that good works will be what results in God's grace for you!

Christianity teaches that God cannot be bought off by humans' good deeds. Rather, the *only* way to be brought into relationship with the Lord is by the blood of His perfect Son, Jesus Christ!

Doubt #7: Is Following Jesus Just All About Following Rules?

I can see how many people think this way. I don't quite agree.

Although there are plenty of times that the Bible tells us not to do something, it isn't the way that we think about it to be. God tells us these things because He knows that only harm will follow. People will look at the times in the Bible where God commands us something or tells us to abstain from sin, etc. He says it because He cares about our well-being and our walk with Him. He doesn't do it because He is a spiritual dictator. My old college basketball coach used to put it this way: "The Bible isn't as much about what not to do, but it's more about what *to* do!"

I'll give you a minute to let that one sink in.

Doubt #8: Why Are Christians Such Hypocrites?

Ooh! The million dollar question! Okay, I am going to give you two reasons why Christians are often hypocrites. One might sound like a cop-out, and the other may be more of what you want to hear.

Reason #1: Even Christians are broken people, being redeemed every day and on their own journey to be more like Jesus.

This could sound like I am trying to make excuses here, but I am not. One thing that we need to remember about pastors, speakers, teachers, prophets, evangelists, apostles, and Christians in general is that they are all still broken people. Think of them as a street that has construction being done and a sign on it that says, "Work in progress." Although we strive to be more and more like Jesus, we are not Jesus Himself. So please give Christians that level of grace. Now, I am not saying to let people step all over you and take advantage of you, because people in church leadership should be held to a higher standard, but please give Christians the kind of grace that you have received yourself.

Reason #2: Christians are often prideful and have the wrong attitude of being "holier than thou."

This is not okay, by the way. I would like to apologize on behalf of the Christians who have acted this way toward you and other people. I unfortunately have encountered Christians like this, and they are unbearable at times. They have what we call a "Pharisee attitude." If you want to know what I mean, go and study who the Pharisees are in the Bible. They weren't very close with Jesus, let's just say.

Even though you may want to hit Play on the song "Apologize" by Timbaland, I am truly so sorry that church folk have hurt you or someone you know and have been hypocritical. I pray that you can forgive us and find reconciliation with the church.

Doubt #9: Why Would a Decent, Good Person Like Me Need Forgiveness?

This is simply answered by a passage in Romans 3:23, where it says, "For all have sinned and fallen short of the glory of God ..." (Romans 3:23). What this and other Scriptures like it tell us is that we all have a sinful nature. The reality is that we are all sinful.

You could be a monk who just lives in the hills and reads your Bible all day (I do not recommend this lifestyle if you are not called to it). But even if you were to do this, you would still need the redemption and sanctification that comes only through Christ Jesus. Why? Well, because although we may be doing the things that good people do in this world, there could still be something we carry in our heart that is sinful in the eyes of God.

I define sin as something that separates us from God and a transgression against God. Sin is a blatant act. But Jesus tosses a "mind bomb" to us when He says, "You have heard it was said, 'You shall not commit adultery.' But I tell you that anyone who looks at a woman lustfully has already committed adultery with her in his heart" (Matthew 5:27–28). That means we can sin even if we don't take up physical action on it. Yikes!

Doubt #10: Isn't the Chaos in the World a Sign of God's Absence?

Yes, it is! Well, sort of. Genesis chapters 3 and 4 teach us that humanity fell away from God and sin entered humanity itself. The effects of this fact are present in every bad thing that happens to people. Death, rape, torture, pain, bloodshed, war, abandonment, brokenness, etc. are all because of sin in our world. But God is still sovereign and not completely absent from this world. What the heck does that mean? It means that although God allows chaos to happen due to humankind's sinfulness, He still reigns above all of that.

God has not completely abandoned humanity, and if you want evidence of that, then look no further than the four gospels of Jesus (Matthew, Mark, Luke, and John). God still loved His creation of humanity so much that He said, *That's enough! I am sending my Son to fix this thing!* (my paraphrase).

And that is what happened. God literally put on the flesh of man and lived the life of a man, lived perfect and sinless, then died a terrible and horrible death as an innocent man for our sins. Then He rose on the third day to entirely defeat sin and death! And that victory is accessible for us through Jesus! So, no, God has not abandoned humanity, because we have the greatest hope in and through Jesus!

SECTION 2: PLAYING YOUR PART

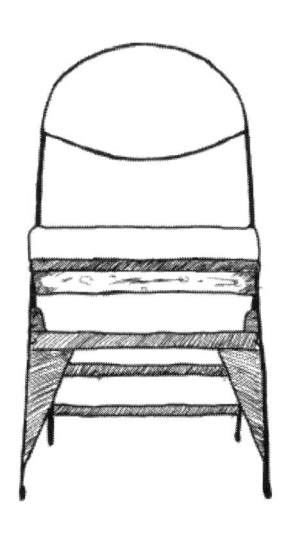

Chapter 5: Healing From Church Hurt

Everyone has experienced a measure of pain from attending church because that's the nature of interacting with others.

—Lecrae Moore

I want to begin the second section of this book with a somber conversation and reminder that many of us have been through some very hurtful times at past churches. It's a sad reality that many churches have hurt and created spiritual trauma in the lives of many.

We cannot shy away from talking about this because not only is it real for many going through this today but it is the true experience of many people reading this too. The topic of church hurt is an eyesore within church history, to say the least, and because it's so uncomfortable for people in the church to talk about, it is often neglected the attention it requires.

The result is that people get hurt from the church, then their experiences are rarely validated, and even if they are, the church never talks about how detrimental those experiences can be to someone's faith journey. Then we have an epidemic of Christians walking away from the church, and deconstructing their theology and belief in God by themselves. Then they may walk away from the faith altogether because, for many, the only solution they see for church hurt is to leave the faith entirely.

Before I began my college basketball career, I had played basketball since I was seven years old. I started in the first grade and continued to play in the children's leagues until everything actually got competitive around the fifth grade. Then I started to play on traveling teams until the seventh grade (my first year of middle school). There I played on the B Team and learned quite a few new skills to help me become more competitive.

Then the next year (eighth grade), I swung between the B team and A team. This was quite the experience because I basically had two different coaches who taught me very different things. I would play a B team game and then go straight over to play in the A team game right afterward. Then my freshman year of high school, I tried out for the team and made the freshman squad. First year of high school, I learned so much about how I needed to get better in my skills. Then my sophomore year, I made the frosh-soph team, where I was an older player. It was pretty frustrating in many ways; however, it was a good experience because I was able to have a new coach nevertheless.

For my junior year, I tried out, but this time I got cut from the team. Cut. Nothing. That's it. No basketball for me. I was heartbroken and my morale destroyed. I thought I was done for and that my playing days were over. So for my senior year, I didn't even try out for the team because I thought I knew what answer they would give me. I honestly gave up mentally. I was so hurt and had my head so down that I thought, *Well, that's it for me! Time to hang up the old Adidas kicks!*

But I couldn't get away from the game of basketball, so I started playing in open gyms in Portland, where I ran into and got connected with a coach of a city league team. He saw me play and invited me to go to a practice with his team. From there, I started to play in that league, where I worked my way up from bench player to a full-time starter. Then after the season ended, he invited me to play for his Amateur Athletic Union (AAU) team that he also coached. I accepted the invitation and played a few months of AAU with his team and enjoyed every minute of it.

Then it was time for me to graduate from high school. I was very mentally prepared to "hang up the shoes," but then I visited Portland Bible College for a tour. I was already planning to attend this school due to feeling led by God to go there, so I decided to go on a tour to the school I was already accepted into. During the tour I had confirmation upon confirmation that this was the school where I needed to go. The final cherry on top came during the last leg of the tour when I was introduced to the basketball team's assistant coach. He showed me around their facilities and the gym, then invited me to an open gym later that week. I went to about three open gyms before the head coach told me that he would like me to join the team because he thought I was a good fit. So I signed my letter of intent, and the rest is history.

I could go into plenty of detail about how crazy my basketball journey was before I even started playing in college, but in short, I had many great and many horrible experiences in the game of basketball. I was hurt by many coaches, teammates, and teams. The problem was not as much about my being hurt. The problem was that I took those past experiences into every new experience I had.

Something my college coach would often say is "I would rather have a player who hasn't been taught very much compared to a player who has been taught something wrong." Why he would say this is because once a person has been taught a certain way, it is more difficult to unlearn that habit and learn a new habit. That brain wave is already there. But when you have somebody fresh, with little past experience, you have a clean and fresh slate to teach them. You have less opposition to go against the new habits that you're trying to instill in them.

This concept relates also to many other areas of our lives too, including how we take our past church experiences with us into our new churches.

Leave Your Chips at the Door

If you're familiar with sports lingo, you have likely heard the saying, *You know, he really plays with a chip on his shoulder!* In the sports world, it's often praised when a player plays with a chip on their shoulder. It typically means that they play with an edge to their game and that they have a serious desire and deep fire to achieve. Everyone loves watching a player who has that chip on their shoulder.

But there is a problem with having a chip on your shoulder. Nine times out of ten, a person has a chip on their shoulder because they have felt wronged by someone at some point. For many athletes, it comes from experiences where they may have been overlooked by a coach or scout, or they felt they were being treated unfairly by their coach for one reason or another. They have this edge about them that says, *I am going to show them! I'm gonna show them what they missed out on. I'm gonna prove them wrong.*

And many players who play with this chip on their shoulder also *live* with this chip on their shoulder!

For me, I had a huge chip on my shoulder. I was overlooked and treated unfairly many times in my life. Before playing in college, I was disrespected and treated poorly by coaches, parents, and teammates. I was overlooked by many coaches due to my lack of size, so I began to have a chip on my shoulder that said, *I am gonna show them that they were wrong!* I started to harbor bitterness in my heart, and I started to take on a victim mentality.

Then I went to play in college, and I took these past experiences of pain and hurt, and I carried this chip on my shoulder into this new team and experience. My freshman year of college brought many trials and struggles, which I handled all with an edge and sort of bitterness in my heart. It was very unhealthy. I am thankful for a college coach who called me out of my mess and challenged me to let those things go. I am also thankful for the Holy Spirit to help me release those things and have forgiveness rather than unforgiveness in my heart.

This issue that I struggled with in basketball is the same issue that many Christians struggle with in the church. Many Christians have been hurt by church leaders (coaches) and fellow believers (teammates). Then the natural coping process that we begin to use to deal with this pain and hurt is that we develop a chip on our shoulder. One that will put us on edge for whatever church we go to next. I cannot stress this enough; this is a tremendously dangerous place to be. It can permanently ruin your outlook on the church, on Jesus, and on the faith as a whole! This is how the Enemy would love for you to be, because you will never truly get connected with the body of Christ with a chip on your shoulder, and that will harm your relationship with Jesus.

Baby Steps to Healing

First and foremost, I want to say something that you might have never heard from anyone else. I want you to know that your feelings of hurt and pain from your past church are valid. You need to know that your previous church experience where the pastor was spiritually abusive and manipulative was *wrong*. Your past experience where the pastor or church leader that you trusted and looked up to ended up having a sexual scandal come out was *wrong*. Where the church leader or member blatantly told you that you did not belong there was *wrong*. If they have never said these three words to you, then I will do it on their behalf: *I am sorry*.

Please forgive them, I know that they may not deserve your forgiveness, but let me tell you two reasons why I am asking you to forgive them anyway.

Forgiveness Is Poison to Your Own Heart

I have heard it said that harboring unforgiveness in your heart is like drinking poison in hopes that it will kill the *other* person. This is contrary to how we often think and feel, though. We think that when we withhold forgiveness toward someone, it hurts them. Sometimes your forgiveness or unforgiveness doesn't impact them whatsoever. It only damages your own self when you choose to not forgive.

Jesus Forgave Us When We Weren't Deserving of It

As hard as it is for us to agree with, it's the truth. God in His might and mercy looked down on us in our sinfulness and chose to forgive us. We turned our backs on Him more times than we can count and disgraced Him every time that He showed mercy, yet He still chose to send Jesus, God in the flesh, to die for our sins. He forgave us when we clearly did not deserve it.

We often think someone should have to earn our forgiveness by their regret and repentance of their offenses. Whether or not someone deserves to be forgiven should not be a qualifier to your forgiveness toward them.

Ultimately, forgiveness is freedom. Think about that. When you have unforgiveness toward someone and you finally are able to forgive them, it feels so freeing to your heart and soul! Because you are releasing their offenses from your heart. Forgiving someone does *not* mean that the offenses did not hurt you or cause trauma there. Forgiving someone does *not* mean that you should return to that relationship like it was before.

Wisdom may say to leave that place and church and find a new church, but it will also say you should forgive that person on your way out. I also don't want to understate how hurt you might be from your previous churches. Pastors can sometimes not understand how much power they have to truly damage someone. So if you are here reading this, and you feel like I am talking about you in this section, please don't skim over it. Please seek God on this and ask Him to help you forgive _____. Ask God to give you the supernatural ability to forgive someone who doesn't deserve it.

If you don't deal with that stuff right now, you will surely carry that baggage into your next church and hold those pastors and church body accountable for something that they didn't do to you.

Sometimes the Most Healing Thing Is a Healthy Relationship

There is an old biblical concept called the kinsman redeemer. We see it in the book of Ruth, where Boaz is Ruth's kinsman redeemer. And we see it also in the Gospels, where Jesus is *our* kinsman redeemer. In short, the idea of the kinsman redeemer was to right the wrongdoings of another.

We see this actually happen pretty often in our modern society. Of course, we don't make it so formal or call it the "kinsman redeemer method." However, it is seen pretty often, especially in the world of dating. For example, we have a man or woman who has some kind of past trauma, maybe even from their childhood. And it is a monster of a problem that is causing some issues in their life as an adult. They have gone to counseling and mentoring sessions with people to help heal and address the issue, but there's still some part of it that's unresolved. Why? Because there are some things in this world that cannot be fully healed until we have something to "repave" those broken roads. In other words, sometimes ... the only way to fully heal from a bad relationship is to be in a healthy relationship.

This is a difficult thing to do for many, though, because this means that you have to put yourself out there again. I see this in many Millenials in fact. We are scared to start dating someone or start a new relationship because we are scared of putting ourselves out there and being vulnerable. We don't want to be hurt again. When you start a new relationship, you are opening yourself up to be potentially hurt. So many people say, *I don't like getting hurt, so I can avoid being hurt if I just stop dating.* Problem solved, right!? Wrong, their past pain still eats at them. Because their only experience is that of a bad, toxic, and unhealthy relationship, they don't know what a good, godly, and healthy relationship looks like, let alone feels like.

So here's my encouragement for you. I know you've been hurt by a church in your past. Your hurt is valid. Your reluctance to go to a new church is understandable. But you must try again. Just like dating, you need to try again. Because sometimes, the fullness of healing from that past trauma and church hurt comes by God putting you in a healthy church, where you can see and experience what real church is supposed to look like. You can do it. Start to look for churches in your area that have a good reputation. Ask your Christian friends which church you should go to. Maybe check out a couple different churches before firmly getting planted into one. Pray and ask God where He wants you to go.

The temptation for you will be to want to go and heal all by yourself, away from the church, but I have never heard of that really working. It is true that your involvement in church may need to be totally shifted or reduced, but please never underestimate how God can use a fruitful and healthy church to restore your trust in the church again.

Chapter 6: Finding Your Home

Surely you know that if a man can't be cured of churchgoing, the next best thing is to send him all over the neighbourhood looking for the church that 'suits' him until he becomes a taster or connoisseur of churches.
—C. S. Lewis

Alrighty then. Queue up the Jim Carrey clip from *Ace Ventura*. It is time to get into my favorite part of this book. This is where you get to actually apply all of this new knowledge and wisdom that you have. Now we get to talk about the main reason why many of you even opened this book. Now we will be talking about getting into a local church and how to go about that

So how do you even go about finding a church that fits you? How do you go about finding a church that lines up with your core beliefs, values, doctrines, mission, etc.? I know that many of you are probably tired of this online-dating style of church searching. *Ooh, this one looks good!* But then you show up, and you don't "vibe" with the place. Or how many times have you been catfished by a church that looks different online than in real life? Regardless of that, I am so excited for you. I believe that God truly has a perfect match for you and your family, whatever season of life you currently are in.

First, you need to understand something that you may not be practicing with this specific topic. A very good piece of wisdom in anything and everything having to do with goal setting is that you need to have a target. You need to know what you are shooting for. Think of it this way: If I were to give you a bow and arrow and I told you to shoot the arrow, the first thing you would likely ask me would be, *Okay, but where am I supposed to shoot it?* That is exactly the point here. Just like shooting a bow and arrow, you need to have a target to aim for when goal setting.

This isn't even a goal-setting book, but there you go. Let's continue. How do we determine what our targets are? We know that we want to find a home church, but what are the determining factors that are important in setting that target?

Your first step needs to be determining your negotiables and nonnegotiables. We all know that it is easier to be told to do something rather than figuring out what to do ourselves, but this is something that you need to do *by yourself*. I cannot help you determine what your negotiables and nonnegotiables are. That's on you and only up to you. However, I will give you some examples to maybe help get your brain pumping.

Examples of negotiables:

- how worship sounds (new songs, old songs, etc.)
- the stage setup
- the sanctuary setup (chairs vs. pews)
- too formal or not formal enough
- literally any type of preference

Examples of nonnegotiables:

- Is the gospel of Jesus being preached? (vs. man's gospel)
- Is this church involved in the community? (Hebrews 6:10; Mark 10:45)
- Is the character of God being represented in the church?
- Are women involved in preaching, teaching, and communicating the gospel? (Just study who Priscilla is in the Bible.)
- Is the fruit of the Spirit present in this church?

So here is a homework break! Let's hit the pause button for a few moments. Go grab a piece of paper and make two lists and title them *Negotiables* and *Nonnegotiables*.

Once you have these lists, you will be better equipped to make any future decisions on where to start being a part of a church. These lists will help you understand the distinction between what is truly important and what is simply a feeling of discomfort, between a frustration and a rational thought, between something biblical and a fleshly opinion.

I Quit!

Raise your hand if you have ever left a church before. Did you leave that church because of a very unpleasant situation? There are plenty of reasons to leave a church—plenty of good reasons and plenty of horrible reasons to leave. I cannot begin to tell you how many conversations I have had with believers over the last several years regarding their frustration and feeling of wanting to leave their church. I've heard it all (totally not exaggerating).

- My pastor doesn't care about me.
- I don't think this church is Spirit-filled.
- The pastor doesn't preach how I like.
- The worship doesn't move my heart.
- I don't feel needed at my church.
- My Pastor is a jerk.
- I feel like if I left, they would be fine.
- I don't feel like I am contributing here.
- This church doesn't align with my core beliefs.
- I don't think the focus/vision/mission of this church aligns with me.
- I don't feel like I'm being fed here.
- The pastor said something hurtful to me and never apologized for it.
- I think the church focuses too much on …
- The church is too charismatic for me.

Do any of those sound familiar to you? Maybe you've heard them before, or maybe you've been the one to say or feel them. Pretty interesting how many of these sentences start with *I* and are *me*-focused.

Can I tell you something challenging and in love real quick? If you ever feel like it's the church that needs to change, the odds are that *you* are the one who needs to change.

This obviously does not apply to every single situation, but the majority of the time it does. Early in my ministry career, I quickly began to get frustrated with some things in my church. We didn't do this, this, and that the way that I believed they should be done. One of those specific examples was around community. I am a very big community-driven person, and I didn't like how we did community as a church. I thought it could be better, and I didn't feel that we put enough focus and intentional effort around the topic. As I continued to get more and more frustrated about this specific thing, I would go to my mentors and pastor friends who didn't have any association with my church (seeking an unbiased opinion), and I unloaded my thoughts to them.

One of my mentors made a comment to me that rocked my inner soul and changed my mindset forever. "Clearly you are passionate about this issue, and you are unhappy with where it is currently at. Have you ever considered that perhaps that is the exact reason why God has you at that church?"

Woah! Boy, did that hit me to the core. He elaborated and explained that perhaps God put me in this church so that I could lead the change that I wanted to see. So. Stinking. Good. And I gotta say, it was convicting! That new understanding took the responsibility off my lead pastor and put it on me. It took the blame off my church and put it on me. It said, *Okay Jacob, if you want to see that happen, then go make it happen. Lead the charge. Be the pioneer to the change that you seek in this church and body.* I have rarely heard something that both convicts me so much and stirs in me, a desire to get up and go.

So when is it okay to leave a church, and when is it not okay? Well, a wise mentor of mine once told me this: "If bitterness is the motive for leaving a church, it will always be harmful and bite you in the butt!"

A pretty interesting way of putting it, but I have heard this said before. The idea is actually based on Hebrews 12:14–15: "Make every effort to live in peace with everyone and to be holy; without holiness no one will see the Lord. See to it that no one falls short of the grace of God and that no bitter root grows up to cause trouble and defile many."

There is something very spiritual about bitterness. It damages the very makeup of someone's soul. It creates a hardened heart. It makes a person be very sharp with their words and hurtful in their tone of voice. It can give someone a short temper. There is *no good thing* that can come from bitterness ... and that includes leaving a church out of bitterness. So my wisdom for you is to avoid this at all costs. If it means that you have to stay at a church longer than you would like so that you may let God heal your heart and take away that bitterness you carry, then it is worth it!

If it comes down to it, always choose short-term pain and discomfort for long-term peace and health.

Chapter 7: Bonding With Your Team

None of us, including me, ever do great things. But we can all do small things with great love, and together we can do something wonderful.
—Mother Teresa

So you found a church and you feel this is the place where you should be. Great! Amazing! Now what?

Well, now is the time to start the process of being planted and taking up a posture of being rooted. But that takes time, and I understand that. Being rooted and planted in a church takes faith that this is where you need to be. It also requires trust in the pastor(s), elders, and every other leader in this church body; agreement with the doctrine, mission, focus, and vision of the church; and commitment to serve those in leadership and those in the community.

All of that takes time. Your first step in this endeavor is to begin learning about your team and growing in relationship with them overall. Remember, we are talking about church in this book but also how the world of athletics can help frame our mindset regarding the former. So when I mention the word *team* in this chapter, I am talking directly about the church body, church leadership, church volunteers, etc. Get it? Got it? Good!

The First Play

Something about me as a person: I am *very* relational focused. I am driven and proactive in making relationships, and I prefer it no other way! This chapter will be more difficult for the introverts out there, and I apologize, but it's worth it. I promise! I have come to the conclusion that although in most settings, it is harder for introverts to make new friends and begin cultivating new relationships, it is not as uncommon as we make it out to be. I believe regardless of personality differences, people build relationships with others when they have mutual interests, attitudes, humor, passions, hobbies, and such. So look in the mirror and ask yourself these things: What am I passionate about? What are my interests? What are my hobbies? Am I a people person or a secluded person? With that information in the front of your mind, you can search for events and groups that you can attend or serve on your new team.

I am passionate about people! Then maybe go serve in your church's outreach events, like the food pantry.

I really like to cook and try new recipes! Perhaps you could use that as a talking point with some people you talk with after church on Sundays. You never know, maybe it could lead to a new ministry opportunity as well. Or even volunteer to make food for your church's youth ministry! I guarantee that they would love that.

I love to watch football! If you love watching Sunday football games, connect and meet some people in your church and set up a day where you all could go over to someone's house or a restaurant after church and catch a game.

I am more of a quiet and mellow person. Make a goal of talking to one person after church every Sunday. Maybe ask a leader in the church if they have a need for someone to serve on the sound team or if there are any areas of the church where you could serve in the background rather than up front.

Baby Steps Are Still Steps Forward

I can remember my freshman year of college basketball and the wild ride that I endured. I came straight out of high school and went to college right away. Just a short three months after graduating from high school and being an eighteen-year-old among young teenagers, there I was on a team that was predominantly twenty-two years olds and older. A couple of my teammates were twenty-five and one was even twenty-six! But there was little, eighteen-year-old Jacob among the grown men!

Pretty quickly, I was given the nickname "Baby Jake" by my teammates. Although you would never catch me arguing about the nickname, I wasn't too fond of it. As I tried to become acclimated and adjust to this new lifestyle, I had many, many growing pains. Not physically exactly, but definitely mentally, emotionally, and spiritually. I had some mountaintop moments, but that first year on my college team, I had many more low-valley moments!

I had moments when I wanted to quit because it was "too exhausting." Times when I felt that I was being treated unfairly, when I was frustrated with where I was in comparison to my teammates, when I felt like others got more opportunities to prove themselves. Times when I felt like I wasn't good enough, when I would question my place on the team, and when I would ultimately seek to understand what my role was on this team. In my first year on this team, I was tested in some specific areas of my life:

- my pride and ego (not being where I wanted to be)
- my patience (especially with other people)
- my willingness (to do things that I didn't want to do)
- my dedication (to work hard, even though I may not see the results immediately)
- my sacrifice (to be a part of something bigger than myself and to play a role that I may not exactly want to)
- my teamwork skills (to sometimes lower myself in order to elevate someone else, which would lead to both of us being successful)

I wish you could see a short film on my first year of college basketball, but the reality is that nobody would watch that. Regardless, I think that it would help encourage someone reading this. Your first year in your new church will likely look much like my first year on that team—a couple of mountaintop moments, but many, many low-valley moments.

That doesn't sound very encouraging, but it is *so worth* enduring those moments! Because when you do, what you learn about yourself, others, and God through those difficult times can grow you and your walk with Jesus so much. The path of growth is not a smooth and easy one; it's the path that is difficult to endure, but when you lean into Jesus during those times, you'd be amazed what He does in and through you. To quote David in Psalm 34:19, "The righteous person may have many troubles, but the Lord delivers him from them all." After that first year on that basketball team, it wasn't all butterflies and rainbows going forward. But I was better equipped to handle what difficulties and adversity I faced in the future because of the work that God did on my heart every day prior! The second year was tough but better! The third year was tough but better! And the fourth year was tough but better!

So as you walk into this new journey with your new church, give yourself some grace. After all, God gives you grace, so who are you to not give yourself grace too? Even if it feels like you are taking two steps forward and one step back, at least you're moving forward. And when you fail and struggle, get back up. Endure! Persevere! It will be worth it!

I Promise I Won't Nitpick

There is a difference between a complainer and someone who actually tries to bring solutions to problems. Be someone who sees the problems and then seeks God for a solution. Please understand and receive this well-backed fact: There will *never* be a church that is perfect and exactly what you want. Every single church lacks. Whether it's strong community, strong doctrine, strong vision, strong small groups, good food (shout-out to youth pastors!), powerful worship, rich diversity, etc. The church that you end up at will be guaranteed to leave you displeased about something. So will you be someone who nitpicks and constantly complains about those areas? Or will you be the one to accept the calling that God's putting in your heart to bring the solution that you know you seek?

In the next chapter, I will talk about the people side of your new church, but keep this at the forefront of your mind: be patient. God's timing is always perfect. And rarely is our timing the same as God's. Surrender that to God and let Him take you on the journey that He has for you and at the pace that He wants to put you in. I don't know who is reading and needs this, but keep the faith! Stay strong! You are at the right church. You are on the right path. It may not feel like that is the place God has called you to and it may feel super uncomfortable being there, but He has you there for a reason. A wise man, a pastor at a young adult service, once told me this, and I want you to take hold of it: "When in difficult times, stop asking God why something is or isn't happening! Instead, ask Him to reveal to you what He wants you to learn about yourself and about Jesus in what you're going through."

Endure and Persevere!

There is a challenging passage found in Hebrews. Hebrews chapter 10 is talking about having a faith that perseveres, but verse 36 says, "You need to persevere so that when you have done the will of God, you will receive what He has promised." Earlier in that chapter, Paul (the author of Hebrews) talks about how we must consider how we meet together and consider how we can encourage and spur one another on in the practice of faith.

The reason for me sharing this passage is this: We must *persevere* through the difficult seasons of life. We typically think if something is hard, then it's clearly not from God. That's very false. When entering into your first year at a new church, there will be times where you may have fear, doubt, lack of faith, unwillingness, and concern regarding this church. I have met only a couple of people in my life that had zero "bumps in the road" in their first year at a new church. It happens! So the Scriptures tell us to endure it and persevere through things like that!

There is a strong theme in the Bible that God encourages His people to persevere. Because he is with us, when we continue through the difficult seasons, we are strengthened and the body of Christ overall is strengthened. So don't give up. Don't interpret the challenges as signs from God that you made the wrong choice. Trust that you heard from God, listened to his voice, and that he led you to where you are now. Whether or not you still harbor doubt and question that statement, have faith that God did lead you here. Weather through the storm with God and let him be your guide through it. It is only for your benefit.

Chapter 8: KYP

It's a close-knit group. When someone in your family is hurting, you hurt.

—Coach Flip Saunders

If there is one thing that I have learned as I have worked in corporate America, it's this: there is an acronym for everything. It's actually pretty overwhelming. The days of social media, instant messaging, and texting have really added to this epidemic. We constantly LOL, BRB, OFC, LMK, etc. But wait, we have CEOs, HR, the IRS, FBI, UK, and USA. It's like you could say it is an "epidemic of acronym overuse"—or you can just call it "EAO" for short. All jokes aside, I want to introduce you to a new acronym to any of you who are not deep in the sports realm. It is called KYP, which means "know your personnel." In the world of sports, what this means is that you know your people. You know your teammates, you know what makes them tick, you know what they are strong at, and you know what they are weak with.

I'll give you an example to hopefully help your understanding.

Let's say you are playing in a basketball game, and you have the ball. The game is all tied up, and you are trying to score but only have three seconds left. You look to your left and see your teammate wide open at the three-point line! You pass to him and he shoots the three. He gets the shot off in time, and the entire crowd raises its voice to start screaming once it goes in! Then you watch the ball as it inches toward the basket, and to your amazement, the ball misses everything, and your teammate airballed the three-pointer by a whole two feet—it wasn't even close to going in! But why? Nerves? Perhaps, but it could also be that the teammate you passed the ball to was the absolute worst shooter on your team. We are talking about the guy who can't make a basket outside of six feet away. *Why was he outside the three-point line? Why was he open? Why did you pass him the ball?*

You see, in this scenario, if you *knew your personnel* better, you would have never passed him the ball when you did. Perhaps you could have got the ball to someone who is a better shooter or even drove it in yourself and got a layup! Knowing your personnel means that you put people in situations where they can succeed and do not put them in situations where they will not succeed. But how does this apply to church?

Well, I believe that we can sometimes have an tendency to place an unhealthy amount of pressure, expectation, and demand on our brothers and sisters in the church. As we continue in this chapter, I want to talk about how we can do a better job at understanding and knowing ourselves as well as the people we serve with. Let's create healthy ministry relationships with our personnel.

DYR—Defining Your Role

It's the word that's in the title of the book. Finding your role in church and in this life hinges on *understanding* your role. As much as I'm sure you'd love for me to just sit here and tell you what your role is, you need to do some searching yourself. I think that is a question only you can answer, and I would be lying to you if I acted like I could do that for you. At this point, I have given you a lot of information; much of it tells you what you're called to do. You are called to be a part of the body of Christ (the church and the local church), serve the body of Christ, and make disciples. But your specific role in all of that is not for me to tell you.

So how can you find that out? I come from the frame of thought that says you cannot do something you haven't defined. Example would be that you cannot be a coffee barista without defining what that role even entitles and means. What are the responsibilities and expectations for that role? I am going to include some different roles that are potentially in front of you. You may not be called to do one or the other, but these are just to help you understand some of the roles within the church and in our faith walk as Christians.

The Coaches (Pastors and Elders)

Many people look up to these men and women and wish that they were in their shoes. Many people see the pastors preaching up on stage and see the kind of pull that the eldership teams have within their churches and think, *Wow, I want to do that!* But what many people often neglect to consider is how many years of life, schooling, being discipled and training it took for those people to be in those places. Most of the time, people aren't put into places as pastors or elders simply because of skill and talent. Usually, they are put into those places because of things they learned over the course of their life, things that cannot be attained in a matter of months. If you are called into the pastoral ministry or become an elder, then pursue those things. Pursue growth, wisdom, knowledge, and experience to back it all up, but never pursue those things out of the motive that wants it because it is "cool." Bad motives may not show up initially, but they will certainly show themselves eventually, and the longer it prolongs, the more damaging it will become for all involved!

The Star Player (Leader on Stage)

The star player is another idolized role that many Christians froth at the mouth for. We look at these leaders who are up on the stage, preaching on occasion, leading worship, doing announcements, etc. It can look so attractive sometimes. Thinking that if we could just get up on that stage, then all of our identity issues, insecurities, and loneliness will magically go away! Sorry to break it to you, but that will never be the case. Just as I said with the coach role, your bad motives and reasons for becoming a star player will come to the surface eventually. And when it does, your pastor or leader will likely address it, perhaps by lovingly removing you from your pedestal.

Now some people are put into positions as the star player because of their skill and talent. For example, your worship leader was chosen to lead the worship team because of their skill and talent. If you cannot hold a note to save your life, or if you cannot play a single instrument, then don't be offended when you are passed over to become a worship leader. Just like in sports, a team's star player has been given the green light for a reason: because they are good, because they are likely the best at what it is that they do. This does not mean that you have less value if you are not the star player, but it just means that you need to not hold yourself to the same expectations.

The Starters (The Leaders of Groups)

We know these people as those who lead the various small groups at our church. The women's group leader, the men's group leader, the community group leader, young adult leader, and any other groups your church might have. These are people who are trusted with a heavy responsibility. These are people the coach calls into the game and who play a part in leading others. These are the people who have accountability to the star players and coach. These are people who are less idolized in our churches because they have roles that are more attainable.

The truth is that the starters are also some of the best people to have speak into your life. If you're looking for a mentor, look no further than your starters in your church. They are usually people who are volunteering their time and serving the church by leading these groups because they purely want to lead people into a deeper walk with Jesus. They are typically easier to meet with and have access to compared to pastors and elders. I kind of think about the starters as the big pillars in a church's foundation. They keep the roof held up, and they can bear the weight of what is being put on them. And they help connect the floor to the roof, all the while keeping those underneath sheltered from the weather outside.

The Role-Player (the Core Volunteer Team)

The role-players are people who are ready at a given notice. Do you need them to fill in for a small group leader one week? They can do that. You need them to take over for the hospitality leader who is on vacation? They are ready and willing. These are people who may not have the most responsibility in the functions of the church, but they are willing to be the hands and feet of the teams. You often will see the role-players behind the stage, taking pictures, or behind the sound booth, running the sound system and words monitor during a Sunday service. Maybe they are the people who greet you as you walk into the church. I would say that most of the volunteers in a church are represented in the role-player category.

The Water Boys or Girls (The Event-Only Volunteers)

The water boys or girls are the people in the church who normally just attend the services. Maybe they are plugged into small groups or community groups, but they don't normally serve in any way. But when you let them know that you are in need of volunteers for the big church outreach that's happening soon, they will be first in line to sign up. These are the people who aren't always serving, but they are reliable and worthy to be counted on by the coach and star players. I have seen many people start out as water boys or girls and quickly turn into role-players because they had a taste of serving the church and fell in love with it. I would recommend that if you're a person who is new to church, you should start as a water boy or girl. It takes pretty minimal commitment, and you might fall in love with serving.

The Team Manager (the Whatever-You-Need Volunteer)

The team manager is often seen as the backbone of the operation of the church. Why? Well, because they will meet every need the church may have. They often will tell the coach, *Send me wherever you need me to be. Whatever you need.* These are the people every coach and star player loves. Actually, everyone loves these people. In my experience, I have seen most of the older saints be in this role—the people who might have grandkids and have been walking with Jesus for many decades.

The team managers are the glue to the operation of the church, the jack-of-all-trades kind, heavily reliable and fiercely passionate to do what needs to be done. They don't get fulfillment by being in front of people and on stage, but rather they get fulfillment by serving the areas that need the most help. They know their role, and they are comfortable in that

Working as a Team

I want to note that not one of these roles is more or less valuable to the team than the others. The water boy or girl has just as much value to the team and aids in the success of the team as the star player. And the role-player is just as valuable and aids in the team's success as the coach! The reality is that what kills the life of the individual and the team is when a person starts comparing their role to another person's role. Comparison kills. It's not worth trying because it's a game that you will always lose!

Also, unlike the world of sports and athletics, in the church you don't need skill and talent in order to have a role on the team (church). Your value doesn't come from how many eyes are on you, and it doesn't even come from how many people you lead to Jesus. Your value comes from the blood of Jesus, and through Jesus you are called worthy. God calls you valuable because you are fearfully and wonderfully made as His child. Period. He thinks you are so valuable that He sent His only begotten Son to live a perfect and sinless life, to die on the cross, bear the weight of your sins, and then rise on the third day to defeat sin and death forever! He did that for *you*! For you who are questioning your own self-worth and value. For you who are feeling like you are nothing in comparison to the worship leader and pastor. For you who feel like you are at the bottom of the food chain. God did that for *you* because He sees you as valuable for being who He made you to be.

SCASG—Seasons Come and Seasons Go

To follow up with the theme of defining your role, there is something unique about people who have a role in the local church. Let's pretend that the lead pastor at your church is named Pastor John. And let's pretend that there is an average church member in your same church named Chris. One might look at Pastor John and Chris and come to the conclusion that those two people have a different role in the church. They would be correct by making that analysis; however, the interesting dynamic about local churches is that rarely will you see someone in the same role for their entire life.

In my personal opinion, they should never be in the same role for their whole lives, either. If you compare this to your job or the small business that you work at, you'll see a different trend. I can look back at some of the past jobs in my life and think of a manager that I had who was the manager for more than forty years! Some smaller churches look this way today, and that doesn't mean that they are wrong for having the same pastor for more than forty years! *Faithfulness* is a very underappreciated character trait of Christian leadership in churches, so I am not belittling that gift. However, you rarely see someone stay in the same role in their church for such a long time. Why is this? Oftentimes, the reason is because God calls us out of seasons and takes us into new seasons in our lives quite regularly.

Just as this book has chapters to organize the different sections, emphases, and themes, you can also think of the different seasons in our lives in the same manner. Some seasons are longer and some seasons are shorter, but that doesn't negate the fact that they exist. How this plays into the understanding of roles in the local church is that Pastor John may not always be the lead pastor. Perhaps next year, he will simply become John. And perhaps in six months, church member Chris will become the new lead usher for the hospitality team. Both of them may be in new roles and new responsibilities but never changing in their value to the church or changing in their value to God. People can watch as a lead pastor, like our beloved Pastor John, steps down from their position to go into a season of rest, and they may come to some strongly opinionated presumptions:

"Clearly he couldn't handle the pressure, so he had to quit!"

"Why did he abandon his people and church!?"

"Why did he leave!? Was there a secret scandal that we don't know about?"

"I'm glad he is gone! I didn't like him anyway!"

"If he is leaving, then so am I!"

What few will see is that although Pastor John was the lead pastor for only a short eight years, he was becoming very burned out, and God was calling him into a new season—rest. Or maybe God calls him into a new season at a different church. Or maybe a new season to plant a church. Or [fill in the blank].

In a situation like this, I would be thankful that Pastor John had the ears to hear that God was calling him to step down, and he actually listened enough to go through with it. There are many people who hear God calling them into a new season and they ignore the call. The effect of this disobedience is that you may overstay your welcome, and that's not a place you want to be. When the hand of God lifts off you in your role, it means it is time to move on. For some, that may mean that it is time to step down from their position of leadership in their church. For others, that may mean that it is time to approach the church leadership about taking on some new responsibilities. This whole topic can be very daunting, but my recommendation for you is simple: Pray, *Lord, give me ears to hear when you call me out of the season that I'm in*. Then *listen* to His answer. That means to actually obey and go through with what He says.

Before we move on, I want to encourage you not to make the same mistake that I've made. During the times in my life when I was praying that prayer of "Lord, help me understand when you're calling me into a new season," I would make a sort of ultimatum with God. I would say, "God, I am not going to move out of this season until you show me what the next season will be and how I will move into it." When you hear that, you might think that it's *so* spiritual and I have *so* much faith to believe that God will give me those two pieces of clarity. But the reality is that I was being an absolute, prideful fool.

To tell you the truth, God may have you move out of the season you're currently in without ever telling you anything else. He may simply tell you,

It's time to go, time to move on, and He may not tell you where you are going. The way our world thinks, people may tell you that it's stupid to move on from some place without having a destination already set in place for where to go next. But that's not how God does things. That is why as followers of Jesus, we need to practice and exercise having faith. It takes faith to listen to God call you into a new season without ever having the details of the new season. Occasionally God will give you those details, but when He doesn't, I encourage you to listen and go through with it even still. I know it is scary to move out of your role anywhere—especially in the church—without having a plan for what to do next, but that is the essence of what it means to be a Christian. Sometimes God wants to know if we will listen and obey before He tells us where to go, because in order to listen, it means that we trust Him and have faith that He will carry us through. Are you all right with only knowing 10 percent of the plan, as long as God is in control?

IWPTMEOP—I Won't Put Too Much Expectation on People

The old saying rings true time and time again within church circles. When serving in a church, "You give an inch and the church takes a mile." This is dangerous, and it drives me nuts that the churches of today constantly do this to our people. It leads to burnout, church hurt, and broken relationships. Why do our churches keep doing the same thing but expecting a different result? When you put an unreasonable or unhealthy amount of expectation on a person, you will consistently be let down. Why? Because you are putting your hope in a *person* rather than on *Jesus*. Now, you should trust people, but you should be well aware that they will eventually let you down, not meet your expectations, and possibly hurt you in return. But continue to trust them (unless there are clear reasons to *not* trust), and put your faith and hope in Jesus rather than the person you are trusting.

Expectations are good, and they can create a space and environment for people to grow, thrive, and rise up to meet a goal. When you have high expectations for people, they are occasionally met with a proactive and eager hunger to exceed those expectations. But high expectations are sometimes also met with doubt, hesitation, and temptation to isolate oneself. This is not healthy to be in that place. So rather than taking away all expectations on that person, maybe take off the unreasonable amount of expectation—but also come alongside them, lift them up, and help them through the challenge! This is called love. This is the Jesus kind of love, the kind that is willing to get down from your "throne," and help someone. Now, in this context, I am speaking directly to church leaders, but for those who are not, this is what you should expect of those leaders who have expectations from you. You should have expectations for your leaders, that they would treat you fairly and lovingly with *their* expectations with you.

BWSMFGH—Boundaries Will Save Me from Getting Hurt

Boundaries are *huge* in relationships, friendships, places of work, and even in church! Boundaries prevent you from getting hurt, and they protect others around you from getting hurt by you! So how do you set up some healthy boundaries in your commitments to serving the church? I believe that you need to be bold and upfront with your church leaders. Tell them straight up and to their face what your boundaries are. Don't apologize and let them make you feel bad for having these boundaries in place. Boundaries create space for people to truly live in freedom and grace to give 110 percent while within the frames of the boundaries set forth. Here are some boundaries that you will need to determine:

- How much time am I willing to commit to the church weekly?
- How willing am I to be flexible?
- How much time in advance do I need in order to be at something?
- What are my limits to commitment?
- If I feel like I am being taken advantage of (in terms of my time), when will I confront my leader(s)?

CYP—check your priorities. What are your priorities in life? Your priorities should involve something along this order (most important first):

1. God
2. family
3. church
4. work

The reason you need to set your priorities in order is because this will be how you keep your head on straight. You might have a list exactly like the one above, but after one year of serving in your church, you might find something is off kilter and you aren't totally sure what it is. Then you can refer back to these priorities and realize that at the moment, the church is taking priority over your family. When that happens, things around your life will be affected negatively. It is a dangerous game to play because you never took the time to set your life priorities and then refer back to it. It's not enough to just set this up, but you need to look back and look back and look back to make sure that it is still true in your life every single day.

GGTRG—Give Grace to Receive Grace

The church should be *the* example of a culture of grace. However, that is not always the case. I am a believer that you should give others grace before they ever give you grace. Because if you are waiting for others to give you grace before you will show them grace, then you will be waiting a while. Also, who is to say that they aren't waiting for you to do the same thing first? So how we break this horrible cycle is to be the first one to give grace.

To add, please do not hear what I am not saying. I've heard it said that grace is mercy, not merit, meaning that it is undeserved. This can be a semidivisive topic due to the amount of scandals that have taken place with pastors in our country. There are people on one side who say, *We need to give them grace and forgive them their sins*, while the other side will say,

They knew better and lacked _____, so no. I forgive them, but that doesn't mean we let them back into the church leadership. Both sides have good points and good hearts, honestly!

Giving grace can sometimes become complicated and situational. For example, there can be forgiveness and grace extended to someone who has done horrible things, but that doesn't always mean that you can automatically trust them now. Sometimes, that trust needs to be earned after something that is scandalous. Let us use wisdom in this.

However, in more common and less dramatic failures, I would recommend you give grace to the people who may not have ever given you grace. The reason that we can even do this is because God has given us grace first! We cannot give something that we ourselves do not have, which is why it is typically difficult for non-believers to extend grace and forgiveness toward people. Part of knowing your personnel means that you know that they will slip up and fail you at some point. You don't have to be a prophet to know that, so have you already thought about how you would respond to your fellow brothers and sisters in Christ? Where would you draw the line? How would you uplift someone? How would you counsel them before they repent and are convicted? How would you encourage them after they repent and are convicted? You should be asking yourself these questions so that when the people around you fail you (and they will), you are prepared to act swiftly in grace.

KYE—Know Your Enemy

In every sport, you will play against an opposing team, a team that wants to beat you and see you lose. The teams that you face off against will think and plan strategically in order to devise ways to beat you! When game-planning for your game or meet against these opposing teams, you normally scout and prepare for your specific enemy. Does the opposing team have good shooters/scorers? Does the opposing team have a really good defense? How does your team respond proactively to counter these things?

How you plan and enact those plans will define how you either succeed or fail in your matchup against your foe. It defines whether you win or lose!

Please don't think for one second that as the church and as Christians, we do not have an enemy and foe. Because we do! And his name is Satan. Some call him Lucifer, the Devil, or the Enemy. Regardless of what you call him, he has a strategic game plan to beat you. The Scriptures say that he comes to "steal and kill and destroy" (John 10:10). The Enemy has plans and strategically will lie to you, manipulate you, tempt you, and try to persuade you into falling. He wants to see your relationship with Jesus no longer exist. And he is capable of defeating you if you let him.

Let's not underestimate our foe and opponent. So how do we combat him? Well, the good news is that we already have victory over Satan because and through Jesus. This means that we are able to defeat the Enemy if we partner with Jesus rather than the Enemy. We should then come up with a game plan to defeat this opponent. Some strategic ways to combat the Enemy, which would ensure a victory over him are:

- Stay fine tuned with your Scripture knowledge (that's how Jesus fought back against the temptations The Enemy threw at Him).
- Stay in community with people who will fight for you spiritually, in prayer.
- Pray regularly on your own.
- Define some accountability partners who could help you when you are teetering and struggling.
- Be involved in community groups, Bible studies, or small groups at your church.
- Recite Scripture when you feel that you're being tempted or attacked by the Enemy (again, this is what Jesus did).

The reason the last one is so important is because our words don't really have as much power as God's words do. So when we recite and speak the Word of God, you can know that will make the Enemy flee!

Chapter 9: Let It Flow

We make a living by what we get, but we make a life by what we give.

—Winston Churchill

For those of you who have experience in sports, have you ever had a game or a meet where you were just feeling it? Like you couldn't do anything wrong? Like you woke up, ate five bowls of Wheaties, and you were on *fire!* There have been times when I would be in a basketball game, and I just felt like everything I shot went in. It's a great feeling.

When I reflect back to my playing days, I can attribute my mental game as being one of my biggest weaknesses. This always eats at me because I knew I was better than I would play at times. Sometimes your biggest enemy is your own mind. It prevents you from doing what you know you can do and need to do because it causes you to hesitate and second-guess yourself. There was a point in my college days that I was playing so tight, and I was so in my own head because I was terrified to make a mistake. During this time, my coach pulled me aside after a practice and told me that I need to loosen up. That I needed to just "let it flow" and stop overthinking everything I was doing.

~~~

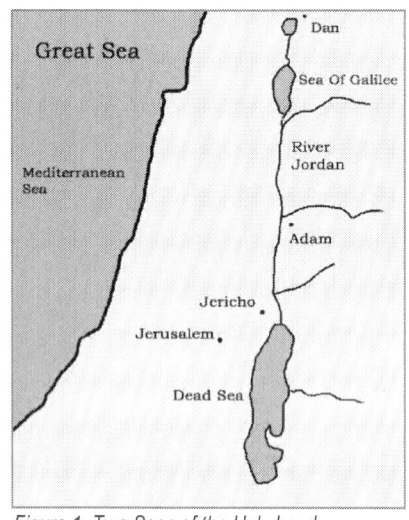

Figure 1. Two Seas of the Holy Land.

This section is one that I'm so excited to teach, because during my time at Bible college, I learned about the lesson of the seas. So let me break it down for you because I think it beautifully portrays our walk with Jesus and the church.

In this illustration, we look at two different seas: one, the Sea of Galilee and the other, the Dead Sea. To give a picture of where these two are located, check out the map [Figure 1].

The Sea of Galilee is mentioned many times in the Scriptures as a place Jesus would go, and many stories are linked to this body of water. Remember that little account about Jesus walking on water? That was the Sea of Galilee. To help you understand how beautiful this place is, look at the lush growth; it is green, full of life, and gorgeous. This looks like the kind of place you would want to go for a vacation, right? It's bountiful with fish, marine life, plants, trees, and more [Figure 2]!

Figure 2. The Sea of Galilee. Photo courtesy of Riley Hamilton.

Then you have another sea just 141 kilometers south called the Dead Sea. When you think of this place, your first thought isn't exactly life. Although this place has quickly become a tourist destination due to its unique salt-to-water ratio that allows people to simply float on the top of the water, this body of water has a rich biblical significance to it.

Examine the picture of what the Dead Sea looks like today [Figure 3]. Notice how few trees surround this water. Notice how there isn't any plants and growth around it? Notice how there isn't much life around it! No wonder they call it the Dead Sea.

So this is the tale of two seas—one of them teeming with abundant life while the other became a tourist hot spot for its unique *lack* of life. But they are only 141 kilometers (87.6 miles) apart.

Figure 3. The Dead Sea. Photo courtesy of Riley Hamilton.

What's the Difference?

So why are they so different, though so close?

Let's start with the Sea of Galilee. The Sea of Galilee is thriving with life due to many things, but one of the prominent pieces is because it is getting poured *into* and it is pouring *out*. Go back and look at that map. Do you see the line that goes into the top of the Sea of Galilee and then out at the bottom? That line is the Jordan River. Sound familiar?

The Jordan River flows into the Sea of Galilee and then flows out of the Sea of Galilee. This constant flow means it is a perfect environment to produce life. Life does not grow and become beautiful by stagnation, but comes only through a *flow* of being poured into and poured out.

Now look at the Dead Sea. As you can see from the map above, the Jordan River flows directly into the Dead Sea. However, there is no outpouring from the Dead Sea. The Dead Sea simply gets poured into and into and into, but never has anywhere for it to pour out. Because of this, it has a very stagnant water flow, which creates a hostile environment for life. Thus it prevents most life from forming there.

Who Is Pouring into You?

If I walked up to you right now and asked you this above question, how would you respond? Would you actually have an answer, or would you give me one of those *Umm, I'm not sure*... There is no shame if you would say that, but I'd love to provoke you to start thinking about how you'd answer. If you don't currently have someone pouring into you, you really should. Let me tell you why:

- It helps you grow.
- It challenges your current mindset.
- It challenges your beliefs.
- It will help you be a better light to those around you.
- It will ultimately help you be a better man or woman of God.

Listening to a pastor preach sermons on a podcast isn't quite what I am talking about here. Many of us could be spoken *to* through a podcast or a spoken word, sermon, etc. However, being *spoken into* means you have someone essentially mentoring you. My old youth pastor from when I was in high school says this: "I've heard hundreds of sermons in my life, but I can only think of maybe two or three sermons that really changed or shaped me. However, I can think of many people who spoke into my life and helped change and shape me!"

Being poured into means that you are *able* to pour out. How are you supposed to pour out when you're not being poured into? How are you supposed to give when you have nothing to give? When you're running on empty?

Being poured into does not happen by accident. There are times when God might orchestrate a relationship in your life for you to start getting poured into, but usually it takes you being intentional about where you invest your time and energy. This means maybe less time hanging out with the guys or gal pals and maybe arranging a time to meet with a mentor weekly. Make yourself available to meet with someone consistently and resist the urge to be flaky or guarded about being vulnerable with them. Let someone serve you, speak into your life and situations, and let someone do life with you in a personal and intimate way! It's seriously such a blessing, and I've gotten through some very difficult times in my life because of those kinds of people.

But How Does This Relate to Me?

So we are talking about two different bodies of water and flow, but how does it relate to you? What do these two seas have to do with you? Well, the Sea of Galilee and the Dead Sea are symbols that can represent two different seasons we are all in.

The Sea of Galilee represents a season when we are getting poured into by someone, a mentor, pastor, coach, etc. Someone who is mentoring, pastoring, and shepherding you, guiding you, and pushing you into a deeper relationship with the Lord. The Sea of Galilee represents a season when you are seeking God, and He is giving you a fresh revelation of His goodness, glory, and words. And then what do you do with all that? Well, you *pour* it all out into other people around you. A Sea of Galilee season represents you praying for people, mentoring a younger person, speaking into someone's life, and giving words of encouragement to those around you, working to serve those around you and in the church.

It represents you getting poured into and then going and pouring out. It sounds a lot like Matthew 10:5–8: "Freely you have received; freely give." The result of this sort of lifestyle is that it is the perfect recipe for growth and life. These are situations and environments where God can work His best for you and those around you.

When you operate this way, people love being around you because you are a beacon of light and life. They can see the life of God flowing through you, and you are acting in and through it. It is simply beautiful.

Then we have the Dead Sea, which represents a season when we are getting poured into by someone, a mentor, pastor, coach, etc., someone who is mentoring and shepherding you, guiding you and pushing you into a deeper relationship with the Lord. The Dead Sea represents a season where you are seeking God and He is giving you a fresh revelation of His goodness, glory, and words. And then what do you do with all of that? *Nothing.* You do nothing with all of that. You just get poured into, poured into, and poured into, and that's it. You just keep receiving from people and God, but you don't pour out into other people.

The result of this sort of lifestyle is a stagnant and unsatisfying life. You can live this way and keep stubborn in your ways, but don't be surprised when you suddenly have feelings of a sort of lifelessness in yourself and something just doesn't feel right. The reason for your struggle and being discouraged is simply because you are receiving from the Lord, yet you do not pour into the people around you.

How the Lesson of the Seas Relates to Church

These two examples of the seasons we can be in are exactly why we need church. Because when you are involved and serving at your church, you have the easiest and most "prime-time" opportunity to pour out into other people. Also, it's one of the best places to go and get poured into. Maybe the pastor's sermon doesn't cut it for you anymore and you need more in terms of being poured into. That's when you seek a pastor or church leader to take you under their wing and mentor, shepherd, or disciple you. There is your source of getting poured into, and then you can get involved with children's ministry, youth ministry, homeless ministry, young adults, Sunday services, etc. in order to pour out. It goes beyond just that feeling of doing a good thing but gives God room to produce fulfillment, life, and abundance in your life. It is about your spiritual life and health. It's so important. Speaking from experience here, it is so worth it.

I pray that we all be more like the Sea of Galilee rather than the Dead Sea!

It's About Serving the Body of Christ

When it comes down to it, it is all about serving the body of Christ. It is a tremendous honor and blessing to do this. But it's also about serving someone else's vision as well. What does that mean? Proverbs says, "Where there is no vision, the people perish" (Proverbs 29:18 KJV). Having vision is so very crucial in our walk with Christ. I understand that many of you reading this are thinking about how you don't even know what you're going to do tomorrow. So let me help you with this concept of needing vision.

I once had a youth leader who was talking to me about how they were struggling because they didn't have any idea what they were called to do, what they wanted to do, or what they were really gifted in. Then I remembered a word that was spoken to me before: "If you feel that you don't have a vision for something, then maybe it is a season for you to serve someone else's vision."

In my selfishness, my knee-jerk response would be to say, *Why in the world would I want to do that? I'm not gonna waste my own time on something that isn't going to benefit me!*

But therein lies the problem. The problem is selfishness. It is pride. I like to look at the story of Abraham (Abram). The Lord gave him a vision for his life and what was to come, but the Lord didn't give that vision to Lot or even Sarah (Sarai). He only gave it to Abraham, so everyone else who went on this journey had to trust in this thing and serve his vision. It's quite difficult to do this because usually you aren't hearing a fresh update from God every single day.

But look at what the vision was and how it played out, and you can see that the vision God gave for Abraham would not have been able to happen without a core group of people who would serve and play a big role in it. For example, if Sarah never bought into the vision that Abraham had, and she just gave up or rebuked him because she wanted to focus on what she needed or wanted for herself, I can assure you that Abraham's vision would have hit a quick and abrupt conclusion.

Now, I also believe that in this specific story, God would have made another way. But I have seen personally some of my old colleagues no longer want to serve someone else's vision, and as a result the vision met a quick demise. And when I am talking about someone else's vision here, I am speaking directly about the kingdom of God and the church. I'm talking about serving your pastor's vision, church leader's vision, small group leader's vision, etc.

Foremost, you must know that you do *not* need to know everything when you serve someone else's vision. Yes, accountability should happen, but maybe you aren't that person that brings that. Perhaps your role in this is to simply serve, give your time, maybe finances, and more. Are you willing to surrender yourself and desire to be a part of something that is bigger than you? Something that God is moving in? God honors godly community and unity, so I believe it is always worth the sacrifice.

Remember, if you don't have a vision for your life right now, then maybe it's time for you to serve someone else's vision.

Resisting Burnout

Story time. There is a young man named Chris who plays for his high school varsity soccer team. It's one day before the final high school game of his career. His team has been fantastic all throughout the year, from defense to offense. Well-rounded and well-coached. Chris is not only a senior captain on his team, but he is ranked nationally as one of the best high school soccer players in the country. Although he hasn't decided on what college to play at yet, he has received twelve full-ride scholarships for different NCAA Division 1 schools. Up to this point, Chris has set his school record for most goals scored in a single season. He has such a high level of endurance and internal drive that he even set the state record for most minutes played in games for the entirety of the season.

This upcoming game is for the state championship, and there is no part of Chris that isn't both nervous and excited. He has replayed different game situations in his head over and over and over until he has memorized what he would do if something off the wall happened midgame. He has been so focused about this game that just a couple days ago, he got in trouble for daydreaming during his science class. He is *ready* for this game. It's all he has been thinking about. He has been preparing his whole life for this moment. Now the day has come, and it's game time. He is nervous, but his preparation, skill, and hunger to win are taking over.

The first half is finished, and Chris's team is losing by three goals. Their coach gives a fiery and inspiring halftime speech, and all of the players start yelling and rallying behind the words spoken. But Chris is starting to hit a wall because he played his tail off the entire first half without subbing out once. He hasn't felt this kind of exhaustion before, but as his hardened desire to win rose to the surface, he pulled himself together once again.

The team then stampedes back to the field, and they fight back into the game. Where they were once down three goals, they are now all tied up with three minutes remaining. Chris's team clearly has the momentum on the field and the crowd can feel it. The opposing bench and student section have a tense anxiety for what might come soon.

Chris has been in a groove, scoring two of the last three goals in the second half, but there is a reason for concern. Chris hasn't stepped off the field once to take a breather (besides halftime). He is beyond exhausted, but he knows that the team's only hope to win this game is for him to stay in the game.

It's neck-and-neck with one minute left! Chris has the ball and is weaving through the traffic of defenders but right before he can get a shot off, he gets fouled. So he lines up for the free kick. He lines up for potentially the game winning shot and the greatest shot of his entire life. But as he is about to take the free kick, he drops to the ground. Everyone freaks out! Parents, coaches, and medical staff start running to Chris. They call 911 and rush him to the hospital.

After a few nights in a hospital bed, the doctors revealed that Chris had suffered a cardiac arrest. His parents were angry, sad, frustrated, and confused about why this could happen. A teenager should *never* have to deal with that. They are too young, too healthy, and with too much energy for that to happen. The doctors ran tests, which disclosed that the reason for Chris's heart attack was the intense overworking of his body.

You see, Chris was only a young man; however, he trained, exercised, and lifted weights every single day nonstop. On top of his normal soccer practices and games, he just never ceased his hard work. Most people saw his work ethic and praised him for it, but it subsequently resulted in him overworking his body.

Chris was released from the hospital, and after spending some time to recover, he realized that all the schools that were interested in giving him a full-ride scholarship to play in college are now hesitant to even offer him a partial scholarship. He feels betrayed, hurt, and confused because not only did he experience something horrible that was the direct result of being overworked but it has now negatively affected his future too.

All right, let's unpack this. First of all, this story is fiction, and Chris is not a real person. So before you try picking apart my story and dissecting its plausibility, understand that it never really happened. Although Chris isn't a real soccer player, he represents many of us who have been burned out from ministry and church. There are some parallels from this story that actually depict where many of us have been or currently are. Some of us have this fiery desire to serve and pour out into our church/community, but we never rest. We never take breaks, and we never take a step back. We never take a breather. We go, go, *go!*

Eventually, our result will be burnout. We may have a metaphorical or even physical cardiac arrest that comes in the form of spiritual burnout. It is dangerous! Don't underplay this issue. Burnout takes out more church leaders and pastors than most temptations and scandals you can think of.

Another parallel is that just like Chris's work ethic was often praised by others, our hard-working, unrelenting servitude to the church is often praised by those around us. Not to say that's bad, but it can lead us to think that that is how we should remain. We take this praise as a sign to pursue deeper and persevere through the spiritual, physical, and mental exhaustion.

The big problem with burnout is that it doesn't only take you out in the moment, like it took Chris out of the game. It also negatively affects and can hurt our future in the church, just like how Chris lost his full-ride scholarship opportunities. Not saying that if you experience burnout, that churches won't want you anymore, but you might harbor bitterness and hold on to some unhealthy things regarding the church. Who's to blame for burnout? Well, that's a great question because it might be something different for different people. But typically, I would say the fault is in these two: you and your pastor or leader.

It is your fault because you can play a victim role in this story, but you could have recognized symptoms of burnout before they resulted in the outcome. You could have stopped doing some things that resulted in what happened. Take some responsibility on this one. That is on you and no one else.

It is your pastor or leader's fault because as your shepherd, they should be very diligent and compassionate about your time and energy and be careful not to overwork you. What is more important than a church service working out? Simple—someone's mental, physical, and spiritual health.

Burnout is real. And it can happen to anyone who is involved in serving (pouring out) in the church (yes, pastors are included in this too).

You can tell I'm spending extra time on this topic, and it's for a reason. If you can recognize that this is a problem, it is easier for you to fix so you don't suffer the same outcome that Chris had. To help you identify if you are at risk of church burnout, here are some symptoms:

- physical or mental fatigue
- lack of passion for serving
- bitterness toward the church (or church leadership)
- resisting direction from leadership
- questioning why you are even doing what you're doing
- inability to say no to church commitments
- rarely or never able to take a day or week off from serving
- feeling of being stressed out or overwhelmed when thinking about your serving area
- on edge with people (short temper)

If you feel that you have half or more of these examples, then my recommendation for you would be to have a real conversation with your pastor or leader.

Take the initiative because your pastor and leaders are not mind-readers, and they need you to tell them when it's too much. So have a sit-down conversation with them and be completely honest and transparent about where you're at. Tell them that you are tired and experiencing some potential burnout symptoms. Tell them that you need to perhaps step back from some things and take a time to rest. It doesn't mean that you'll never be able to serve again, but you need to refuel.

Most pastors and leaders will totally respect your decision. (Well, at least if they are a good pastor or leader, they will.) And they should help you game plan a return to action as well. When having the conversation, it would be a good idea to set a date to return to serving in your mind.

This conversation might feel uncomfortable, but let me tell you something. This will save you from so much hurt, pain, struggles, and spiritual, emotional, and mental damage. It is so worth the uncomfortable conversation; in fact, it shows your maturity as well.

How you recover from seasons and moments of burnout are not as easy as I'd like to tell you, but here are some things that will certainly help you recover from being burned out:

- Practice great self-care (eat well, sleep, enjoy life, fun activities, and spend time with Jesus).
- Set realistic expectations for yourself (expect your leaders to have these as well).
- Set boundaries with your serving (learn to say the word *no*).
- Know your worth (your value is not in what you do, but who you are as a child of God).

Learn from the past and set up new rules and systems for yourself to reduce the potential of being burned out again.

I want to finish this thought with one thing, and that's it: Please don't let yourself get burned out. Burnout is the number one killer of ministers and church people across our country. It is a top reason why people leave a church and never serve again. It is so damaging to you as a child of God, and I want better for you! God wants better for you! The church service will go on, so prioritize that you guard your own heart over a service!

Chapter 10: Who Got Next?

God put us here to prepare this place for the next generation. That's our job. Raising children and helping the community, that's preparing for the next generation.

—Dikembe Mutumbo

You made it. The last chapter of the book. I was praying on how to conclude this conversation about all of this, and I couldn't determine a better way to finish than by giving us all direction on what is next—or rather, who is next.

In sports, there is an interesting thing that happens almost every season. Whether it's high school, college, or professional sports, you will have a moment every season where there is a sort of handing off the baton. The older players are on their way out, and the younger players are next in the line to take control and charge of the team going forward. The change is unavoidable. Every player will be the young player and eventually become the older player who is starting to exit and transition out from the team.

The best teams do the transition exceptionally well, and the bad teams handle it horribly. The good teams start this transition period fluidly and with intention. The older players who equip their younger players best are the ones who start to raise up leaders as soon as possible. In an example of college, the sophomore player is pouring into and raising up their freshman players! You may not be an old experienced player, but you can still do your part in this transition. In fact, I have seen much success in teams that operated that way, because it adds to the value of those sophomores and even juniors. The point is that you shouldn't wait until your last year to begin to raise up the next generation.

I also love this concept because this ensures that the team has success for longer than just the four years that a player is on the team. You can look at teams that have ongoing and continual success for several years, and that accomplishment can be attributed to their ability to handle this transition. So how can you be ahead of the curve in raising up the next generation to take over this team that we call the church?

This is probably my favorite part of the book (have I said that before?) because this is where we get to talk about the next generation. As I have been writing this book, I have been serving at my church as the youth pastor, where I constantly work directly with the next generation. And let me tell you, it is simply my favorite thing in the world! God has given me a huge heart for the youth of today, and I love them! I want what God has for them, and I eagerly desire that they love Jesus and walk with Him for the rest of their lives. This chapter will help guide us to better assist in possibly the most important part of this topic, which is the handing of the baton to the next generation of Christians.

Who Are We Talking About?

I want to clarify who it is exactly that we are talking about, and that is the group of ages one through eighteen. Maybe more specifically, I want to talk about high schoolers (ages fourteen to eighteen) because they are quite literally in the final stage of being children.

As I am writing this book, the next generation that I am referencing is called Generation Z, or Gen Z for short. Personally, I *love* this generation! As a Millennial myself, I get annoyed with my own generation about many things, but I do have a lot of hope for us. Even more so, I really have hope for the Gen Zers!

If you talk with adults or check social media, it is pretty easy to pick on and get upset with Gen Z, but let's be real here. No generation comes out the way it does by accident or happenstance. They become who they are due to the way they were raised (look in the mirror, my friends) and due to the circumstances and situations of their world. This generation has some wild things that they have had to deal with already: a worldwide pandemic (COVID-19), a mental health crisis (overwhelming amount of reported depression, anxiety, and suicide among youth), racial tension, political division, several humanitarian crises, and a society that is severely toxic, polarized, and volatile.

I look at the things that are staring at these teens face-to-face, and yes, we have all lived through these things, but can you imagine being a teenager during these times? Already dealing with identity issues, puberty, and just normal growing pains (physically, emotionally, mentally, spiritually), trying to find yourself as an individual. And then throw all of these real-world issues onto them. Yay for Gen Z, am I right?

Why do these kids act crazy? Why do these kids have anxiety and doubt? Why do these kids have issues trusting people? Why don't they listen to me? Why do these kids act the way that they do? Why do these kids act like they know everything? Well, it's pretty simple when you look at the broader picture. The world is really toxic and messed up, and more than ever (that I have seen), we are pushing these problems onto our children and telling them to have an opinion on them and deal with it.

Let's not get caught up in the weeds of why Gen Z is the way they are, but let's talk about what to do from here.

That Is Not My Job!

I can already hear some people thinking, Well, I get it ... but fixing the next generation is *not my job*. I say this in love, but here is my response to those people: I'm glad all of your teachers in school did not say, *That is not my job*. I'm glad your pastors didn't look at your faults and say, *That is not my problem*. I'm glad Paul didn't look at the churches in Corinth, Philippi, etc.

and say, *That is not my job.* I'm sure glad the people in history who were self-sacrificing throughout their lives for the betterment of others didn't say, *That is not my job.*

Oh man, I'm sure glad Jesus didn't look at the brokenness of humanity and say, *That is not my job!* I'm sure glad He didn't just give up and stop caring about the next generation of broken people.

I take this thing very seriously! We are not only presented with the ability of helping the next generation, but it is actually our responsibility to do so. That doesn't fall on anyone else but you and me. All of us have that responsibility and *it is our job!* The reason there is a lot of brokenness in every "next generation" is because of older generations of people who don't take their protection, guidance, and care seriously. They don't realize the effect of their teachings or lack thereof.

But don't listen to me rant about this, let's look at what the Bible says on the issue. Asaph, the author of Psalm 78, says this:

> My people, hear my teaching; listen to the words of my mouth. I will open my mouth with a parable; I will utter hidden things, things from of old—things we have heard and known, things our ancestors have told us. We will not hide them from their descendants; we will tell the next generation the praiseworthy deeds of the Lord, his power, and the wonders he has done. He decreed statutes for Jacob and established the law in Israel, which he commanded our ancestors to teach their children, so the next generation would know them, even the children yet to be born, even they in turn would tell their children. Then they would put their trust in God and would not forget his deeds but would keep his commands. They would not be like their ancestors— a stubborn and rebellious generation, whose hearts were not loyal to God, whose spirits were not faithful to him.
> (Psalm 78:1–8)

God cares a *lot* about the next generations! Which means that He cares a *lot* about Gen Z! Which means that *we* need to care a lot about Gen Z. Let's not be foolish and ignore our descendants. Let us be people who pour our everything into the youth of today so that they might be better equipped to walk this life in a way that glorifies Jesus and grows His church.

What Do We Do About All This?

I hope by now you're convinced enough to do something about this, so assuming you are, what do we actually do to affect the next generation for Jesus? I understand that many of you reading this are from varying age groups and generations yourselves. I understand that it is much easier to connect with today's youth if you are in your twenties. And I definitely understand that the fifty-plus year olds reading this have a much harder time connecting with today's young people. But fear not; I will equip you all with some practical tools that can help in this endeavor.

Can I Get Some R-E-S-P-E-C-T?

In the spirit of Aretha Franklin, I believe that the way for us to move forward in building up the next generation of the church is to give them some R-E-S-P-E-C-T. Of course this acronym stands for something, so here is what it means.

R = Respect: The R stands for respect. I think it is likely the most important letter because you cannot get anywhere after this without respect. Respect is the only way to build any sort of relationship with young people. It's the first step, and honestly, it's the reason why there aren't as many adults who have real voices in children's lives as there should be. Many adults have a problem respecting children. We demand respect from young people because we've been told *Respect your elders*, but we hardly ever respect today's youth ourselves.

But why? I think it is because we see a correlation between respect and agreement. We think that respect equals agreement, however respect does not mean that you have to agree with someone and their life choices. You can respect someone while disagreeing on everything. Respect means that you hold high regards to someone or something. *If you have something that you value, you will respect it.* And the thing about young people is that most of them will never listen to a person (adult especially) that doesn't give them respect. And if they do listen, they will likely do it reluctantly. If you ever wish to have a voice in a young person's life, you will first show them respect.

E = Embrace: The first E stands for embrace. We need to embrace our young people because (let's be honest here) the large majority of them are dealing with some serious struggles in their young lives. Whether it's issues with identity, sexuality, addiction, temptations, anger, bitterness, envy, impurity, idolatry, unforgiveness, etc., it is all very heavy stuff.

We need to have some empathy for these young people and validate that what they are going through is difficult. As my life has gone on, I've seen many older people *invalidate* the struggles of the youth of today. I've heard the old *You think you got it bad? Try getting kicked out of your house at age 16 because ...* or *You're depressed because you don't have any friends? Try getting sent to a war at age eighteen! Then come talk to me about being lonely.*

I have a strong opinion on this—and to be honest, you might be right; maybe you did have it worse than the young person you're talking to, but oh my goodness! Do you have an empathetic bone in your body? It's so insensitive to tell someone that their pain and struggles are not legitimate. The battle is not whether you are right and they are wrong; it's about whether you can show compassion to people when you don't understand what they are dealing with!

I look at Jesus, and I think about how He really sat there, listening to these people talk. As if He didn't already know what they were going through. I think about how Jesus could have responded to many of these people and could have said, *You think you have problems!? I have to go and die a horrible death because of you!* But He never really did that. He listened, and the Gospels even tell us that He was "moved with compassion" toward many people.

That is such a powerful statement to me. How many times in our busy lives are we "moved with compassion" for people? So what I mean by saying that we must embrace our youth of today is that we need to support and love them. Show compassion for them. Show them that we hear their problems and we validate them. We don't belittle or talk down about them or what they are dealing with. We say, *Wow that's a lot! How are you doing with all of that? Are you doing okay?* And when they open up and reveal their struggles, we embrace them in those moments, rather than respond in a very holier-than-thou way.

S = Serve: The S stands for serve. I want to teach us all a biblical concept right now. It is called serving those who are considered "below" us. First, let me show you were we get this idea from:

> It was just before the Passover Festival. Jesus knew that the hour had come for him to leave this world and go to the Father. Having loved his own who were in the world, he loved them to the end.
>
> The evening meal was in progress, and the devil had already prompted Judas, the son of Simon Iscariot, to betray Jesus. Jesus knew that the Father had put all things under his power, and that he had come from God and was returning to God; so he got up from the meal, took off his outer clothing, and wrapped a towel around his waist. After that, he poured water into a basin and began to wash his disciples' feet, drying them with the towel that was wrapped around him.
>
> He came to Simon Peter, who said to him, "Lord, are you going to wash my feet?"
>
> Jesus replied, "You do not realize now what I am doing, but later you will understand."
>
> "No," said Peter, "you shall never wash my feet."
>
> Jesus answered, "Unless I wash you, you have no part with me."
>
> "Then, Lord," Simon Peter replied, "not just my feet but my hands and my head as well!"

Jesus answered, "Those who have had a bath need only to wash their feet; their whole body is clean. And you are clean, though not every one of you." For he knew who was going to betray him, and that was why he said not every one was clean.

When he had finished washing their feet, he put on his clothes and returned to his place. "Do you understand what I have done for you?" he asked them. "You call me 'Teacher' and 'Lord,' and rightly so, for that is what I am. Now that I, your Lord and Teacher, have washed your feet, you also should wash one another's feet. I have set you an example that you should do as I have done for you. Very truly I tell you, no servant is greater than his master, nor is a messenger greater than the one who sent him. Now that you know these things, you will be blessed if you do them." (John 13:1-17)

What Jesus did here is multifaceted and has many meanings, but what He did here was also very symbolic. The Savior of the world got down on His knees in a lowly place and washed the feet of the men that He walked with. You can think of it like this; your boss at work saw that you were working hard and getting sweaty because of the hard work you've been doing. And when your boss saw that, he went and grabbed a water bottle with the fancy straws and a damp towel and came over to pat dry your sweaty forehead and give you some water to drink. Then your boss said, *Tell me what you need! I will cover it for you!* You feel honored, you feel respected, you feel that you matter to your boss, and you feel that you're valued by your boss.

This is how powerful it is when we serve our young people. *All that "serving" is, is meeting the needs of someone else.* The temptation is to look at the young and dumb teenagers around us and say, *Pft! When are they gonna grow up!* But while we are sitting there saying that, we could put ourselves in a lowly position and think about how we have been in those shoes before in some way, and that in our serving them, we are showing that we care and are invested in them as a person.

Before we move on, I'll give you some examples of easy and not weird (this is important on this one) ways to serve the young people in our lives. Here is a list of eight ways you can simply and easily serve a young person:

1. Pray for a young person (in person or not).
2. Serve in the youth ministry at your church.
3. Serve in youth ministry events (cooking, chaperone, drive, etc.).
4. Meet weekly at the local coffee shop (mentorship).
5. Meet the financial needs of a young person (help pay for youth ministry camps, sports, etc.).
6. Make your skill set accessible to your church youth ministry (example: A coffee making workshop).
7. Speak into their lives (give wisdom and advice).
8. Create a new group at your church that bridges the gap between older and younger people (Pray on it and get creative! There is no one-size-fits-all on this).

I want to make a quick note, that when serving young people, you need to remain above reproach and be kept accountable because this is an area that can quickly lead to some very bad things. I will go into more detail in a couple pages though, so just hang tight.

P = Pray: This one I don't quite feel like I need to go into great detail on, but let's go over it real quick. Prayer is an essential part of every Christian's walk with God, but it is also an amazingly powerful tool that we have. Prayer is so powerful because of a handful of reasons, maybe most importantly because when we pray, we are saying to God, *I cannot do this, it is out of my control. I surrender my hope of my control and seek you in this topic.* When we lower ourselves and elevate God, it's a recipe for success and healthiness! When we pray, we are admitting that we cannot do something and that God can do something. Prayer is important, too, because it is our communication tool to speak with our Creator and Savior. Prayer energizes the believer, and the Holy Spirit can stir up a fire inside that person to seek and go after Him even more. Consistent prayer can release the blessings of God onto you (Matthew 6:6). Prayer also results in God creating change in our lives. James 5:16 says, "Therefore confess your sins to each other and pray for each other so that you may be healed. The prayer of a righteous person is powerful and effective" (James 5:16).

I could go into all sorts of reasons why we should pray and how it is powerful, but that's not my point here. If you'd like to learn more, please check out some resources online and find some good books on the topic. But my point here is that being in your prayer closet and lifting up a young person in prayer is an amazing way of being involved in their lives without having to physically be with them. Sometimes you might need to pray for them in person, but this is something that can be done at home or in the car by yourself.

I can genuinely say I believe I'm where I am in life because of God's grace *and* the millions of prayers from my mom, dad, grandma, family, friends, and many others. The prayers they had covered me with in my youth protected me from experiencing and dealing with things that I never had to suffer through. I still had a difficult life, and it was patchy for sure. But hey, I love and pursue Jesus more and more every single day. That is something I don't take for granted. And I am so thankful for that.

E = Encourage: The second E stands for encourage. Encouraging someone can mean something different to different people and can look different to different people.

When I was in college, I had a basketball teammate from Florida I would butt heads with occasionally. He was a very blunt person and would call you out in the open about your mess. And he wouldn't usually wait, either. If he saw you do something, he would say it right on the spot. This rubbed me the wrong way and really frustrated me at first. I had all sorts of thoughts and opinions about him, but as time went on and I learned more of his heart for people and me, I started to understand him and why he would do this. To him, he was encouraging me to be better, but to me, he was being an annoying, hypocritical, nitpicker. I began to understand that he was saying those things and doing those things because he actually cared about me and my growth.

This is just one example of how encouraging someone to be their best self can sometimes look different from how you would personally do it. But it is also a beautiful example that encouraging someone doesn't always mean you shy away from laying into them about their failures and shortcomings. Obviously, this needs to happen in love! I am a firm believer that you can't fix something if you don't acknowledge that it even exists. How are you supposed to fix that broken pipe under your sink if you don't acknowledge that it is leaking everywhere?

When confronting someone with their sins and shortcomings, it doesn't mean that you yourself are perfect, but it helps someone see that they might have a problem they don't know is there. Encouraging someone means that you verbally speak with them. It implies that you have a relationship with that person too because you usually can't quite encourage someone that you don't have an existing relationship with. So build a relationship with someone and encourage them. Tell them what they are good at; tell them what God says about them; tell them that you love and care about them. And at times, tell them in a loving way where they need to improve. These things are not only key in developing and growing an individual but they are necessary in having a mentor relationship with a young person.

C = Cover: The C stands for cover. This is a weird word to use here, but let me explain to you why I chose cover. Think of it like an umbrella. Try to picture this real quick: I am from the Pacific Northwest where rain is as dependable as death and taxes. Although many local people here do not actually use umbrellas, what is the point of using one? The point of using an umbrella is to protect something from getting wet and nasty. To protect something from the elements. When you dress up all fancy, you use an umbrella because you want to cover from the rain to protect your clothes from getting ruined. In short, we use an umbrella to cover and protect the things that we care about. This is the same mentality we must have when talking about the next generation. It is our responsibility to cover and protect the very precious thing (young person) that we care about.

Covering somebody also requires us to keep that person accountable. It is on you and me to make sure that they do not stumble and trip up. Now

I am not saying that they are not responsible for our own actions, because everyone is responsible for their own actions! But I think of it like this: When I was in student leadership at my old college, one of my fellow student leaders said this: "We need to think of things as a group. I may not be struggling with looking at pornography, but if just one of the guys in this dorm struggles with that, then it means that I also struggle with it."

This mentality shook me! It's easy in life to look at others and say, *Wow look at their problems! Glad I'm not dealing with that*, and move on. But when we are able to look at them as brothers and sisters in Christ and take on their burden too, we can move forward by doing life with these people!

This is key when talking about the next generation because we are able to cover them with love and grace when they mess up. Then we can help them move forward and walk out of the problems rather than wallow in them. Being a covering for someone basically looks like what parents are to their children. When you are a parent, you have this covering over your child that will always be there for them. A covering that tells them they might go out and get in trouble or hurt, but they are always welcome back to the arms of their parents, always welcome back to the loving grace that is their covering.

T = Teach: The T stands for teach. The final letter is likely the one we've all been waiting for, because how many times have we adults been disrespected by some kid where we wanted to teach them a lesson!

Oh yeah, little punk? Wanna say that again? Let me show you how to respect your elders!

Teaching is threefold; it is to educate, motivate, and discipline. Educating is the primary function of teaching someone anything. If that person does not retain or keep the given information, then did they ever actually learn it? In the United States, we can think that the only place where we can learn is in school. Not only is that a lie but we also believe the fallacy that we can only learn between the ages of one and twenty-two, which is also a lie. We should and can learn at all times, at any place, and at all ages.

Education is giving someone else knowledge of some kind in the forms of intellect, wisdom, advice, opinions, and so on. The very cool thing about being a Christian and teaching someone something is that we partner with the Master Teacher, Jesus. We can learn so much about effective ways to communicate knowledge and wisdom by simply looking at how Jesus did it. His teaching tools and styles are still used today. Let's not try to reinvent the wheel on this, because it still works.

It is the responsibility of the teacher to also motivate the student. How you motivate the students will look different based on every student. Often teachers will incentivize the students to do the work and retain the information; however that may not and does not always work. So what do you do then? What I have found success in, especially with young people, is to make it exciting. That may not mean that you have flashing lights, fog, and loud music; it could simply mean that you express your *own* excitement on the topic.

An example of this is when I get the honor of preaching the gospel to people. When I get to speak and preach or teach a message from the Bible, you can *know* that I am going to be passionate and love the topic that I'm speaking about. My eyes get big, I get louder, I move a lot more!

I'm not saying be like me, but it's honestly human nature. People act differently when they are talking about something that excites them. So express that level of enthusiasm when teaching someone something. Don't try to uphold a stoic personality when talking about the things you get excited about. When communicating with the next generation, they will listen more intently when they can tell you are passionate about the things you speak about.

Last, teachers need to discipline their students. Most of the parents reading this are like *Yes! Amen*, but if you're like me, I sort of cringe at the idea of confronting young people with discipline issues. This is an area I am currently growing in and getting better with because this certainly must happen. It's so much easier to ignore, give grace, and move on rather than confront the problems and address them. But it isn't that easy. Young people need to learn. And they need to be told when they are in the wrong.

When you are presented with a situation where you need to address a discipline issue with a young person and you need to bring some direction, you want to be aware of how far you can go. Because, simply, there are limits. Back in the old times, teachers at schools could spank kids. That doesn't really fly anymore, though, and parents are the only ones who would have the ability to really do that.

You need to know your limits and boundaries because you could potentially end up in a very bad position if you step out of line. So first, assess how much of a reach you have in terms of discipline. Likely the most you could do is to have a firm conversation about how *That wasn't cool and you need to stop doing that*. If it persists, you might have to call in the big guns, which are the parents or guardians. Nothing will make a young person upset with you quite like the old *I'm gonna tell your parents*. Regardless of this, there are times when getting the parents or guardians involved is necessary. So use wisdom and don't hesitate to do so.

Disciplining a young person is also important because it protects the boundaries that you have with them. With no rules, there is chaos. And if a person doesn't listen and abide by the rules, then they need to be corrected and disciplined. Perhaps that sounds a bit harsh and a tad authoritative, but it is truthful. It's difficult, but it's how we learn from the past.

Now to recap, what R-E-S-P-E-C-T stands for:

Respect
Embrace
Serve
Pray
Encourage
Cover
Teach

Stay above Reproach

Since we are spending this final chapter talking about being involved with the next generation (youth/kids), then we *need* to talk about this. Sadly, there is a very real temptation that plagues humanity called sexual immorality. Specifically within this conversation, it comes in the forms of having inappropriate relationships with children. It is horrible and despicable! But we need to talk about the elephant in the room because there are right ways of relating to minors, and there are some very, very wrong ways!

Let's begin with some boundaries, shall we? Keep boundaries and rules with how you interact with young people. I am talking about rules that you have for *yourself*! Here are some examples:

- *Never* be alone (one-on-one) with a child.
- Have a relationship with the young person's parents or guardians (they need to know who you are, trust you, and have your contact information).
- When you do meet with a young person in group settings, make sure there are other people who know when you meet and make sure they know where you're going as well.
- *Never* meet with a student without another person of the same sex as the student being present.
- Exercise wisdom with topics discussed. Talking about the birds and the bees with students is totally unacceptable. Confirm with others (maybe even their parents or guardians) whether the topic discussed is appropriate.

FRAGILE—Handle with Care

When working with the next generation of the church, we need to be on the same page on something: We have the power to completely destroy someone's life. I know, very dramatic and intense, right? But it's incredibly accurate!

Regardless of who you are and what your relationships with Jesus and with young people are, you have the power to turn someone off about Jesus—potentially forever. Think about that for a minute. You say the wrong thing, do something hurtful, or cause severe trauma in a young person's life, and you very well might create a divide in their relationship with Jesus forever.

Does that scare you? Good. Does that freak you out? Good. It should. Because we are talking about children here. What does Jesus say about how much He loves these people? Jesus says this:

> He called a little child to him, and placed the child among them. And he said, "Truly I tell you, unless you change and become like little children, you will never enter the kingdom of heaven. Therefore, whoever takes the lowly position of this child is the greatest in the kingdom of heaven. And whoever welcomes one such child in my name welcomes me. If anyone causes one of these little ones—those who believe in me—to stumble, it would be better for them to have a large millstone hung around their neck and be drowned in the depths of the sea." (Matthew 18:2–6)

Yeah, that's the words of Jesus, not me.

One thing to note here, though, is that Jesus is not exactly speaking about a literal child in this passage, but rather, a spiritual child. Sometimes a spiritual child could also be a literal child, but this passage is talking about spiritual children. Nevertheless, He seems pretty intense and serious about taking good care of the children. So let us be sure to take this thing very seriously, please. I've heard so many stories about fathers who have done severe and drastic things to protect or even avenge their children when wrongdoings have happened to them. Just imagine what our Heavenly Father would do if we commit wrongdoing to one of His children. That's enough to instill a healthy amount of godly fear right there.

When we understand the weight of what God calls us to, we understand the immense pressure and grace that we must carry—a grace that only God can give us.

Conclusion

The mission presented to us—living life as a Christian—is not easy but it is promised to be worth it. Not only that, but God promises that we have an Advocate with us. God has not and will not abandon you. After reading this book, I truly pray and hope you have not only been personally encouraged but you also feel more equipped and well resourced to successfully live this life of a follower of Jesus. I try to remind myself every single day that I would never be where I am in life if it wasn't for the church community and godly people who have pushed me deeper and helped guide me on my path towards God. Not only does God walk by our side but He gives us amazing and godly people to also do life with—and they reside in the local church! We cannot abandon that.

Remember that God speaks to us through three different ways:

- through His Word (The Bible)
- through personal revelation (to you individually)
- through other people (example: prophets, pastors, etc.)

My hope is that you would not forsake or give up on the latter of those three. I know there are many Christians and churches that have let people down and actually caused real hurt or trauma to those individuals. It breaks my heart. It angers me more than I can explain. But please know that there really are good people out there in the churches. People you can trust, people who can help you heal, people who can encourage you to dive deeper into your relationship with Jesus.

I know it's easier said than done when I tell you to trust people after you've been severely hurt by people you've trusted in your past. However, I can speak from experiences in my own life when I trusted the people closest to me in my family, as I should, but I have been traumatically let down. Yet I didn't stay in the pit of ash. I trusted in God, and I let Him pull me from those ashes! Let Him heal the broken pieces in my heart. Now today, I can trust people, and when they do let me down, I am not shaken or rattled, because I didn't put my faith and hope in them. I have my faith and hope in Jesus, rather than man. When you put your faith and hope in a human, you are guaranteed to be let down at some point. But when that hope is in Jesus, you will never be let down!

This book has been a long time coming. I started writing in 2017 and worked on it very sporadically. Four years in the making, and I cannot tell you how excited I am to be finally able to share it with you. So thank you for sharing in this experience. This book stemmed from a desire to help people who feel isolated in their faith walk. To help you understand you're not alone and that God has purposefully created a community on this earth to help you in this journey. I am passionate about this because I've felt alone before, and I know how harmful and detrimental it can become to an individual.

I realized that I was blessed to have also lived in the athletic world for almost my entire life, and looking back, I can recount numerous things that I have learned about my relationship with Jesus and as a Christian from just the game of basketball. I know it's crazy, but you'd be surprised how much we can learn about being a Christian from simply playing a sport. I understood that many people haven't had the experiences in sport that I have, so I wanted to share some of these concepts that helped me understand things clearer, especially regarding the church body. Because this life as a Christian can be very difficult, specifically for those who are new to the faith. So if you don't take anything away from this entire book, please know this one thing...

You are loved! And you are not alone in this journey.

CONCLUSION

I may have never met you, and I may not ever, but know that I am praying for you: That you would find a community and a church that you can fall in love with. That you would find people you connect with yet who will also give you the tough love you surely need at times.

As long as you are on this earth and breathing in air, God certainly has plans for you, and they are plans for your *good* that will surpass your understanding and expectations. Once you hop on the wave that God puts in our lives, it's a wild ride. It's one that I hope I never stop living because it is so fulfilling and gives me life. When I can do all of these things, it allows God to move me into my purpose.

I cannot overstate how important simple obedience is. It is a protective covering over us, and when you obey the Word of God, watch Him do amazing things in and through you. Only then are you following God His way, rather than following God your way.

So I hope this book has blessed you and helped you with finding your place and role in your church and in this life as a believer. The journey will certainly present more challenges every day you continue, but have faith in God that He is guiding you and pursue Him with more fervency every day.

I pray that you get connected with an awesome group of Christians in your church and that they support you in times of weakness and challenge you to grow in your faith. You can do this. And when you understand what your role is in all of this, it is so much less stressful and much more enjoyable. God bless!

~ NOTES ~

[1] A.W.Tozer, *Tozer on Christian Leadership: A 366-Day Devotional*. (Cam Hills, Pennsylvania: WingSpread; Reprint edition, 2007).

[2] Wayne Jackson, "What Is the Meaning of Ekklesia?" *ChristianCourier.com*. Access date: October 18, 2021. https://www.christiancourier.com/articles/1500-what-is-the-meaning-of-ekklesia.

[3] John R.Kohlenberger III, *The NIV Exhaustive Bible Concordance: A Better Strong's Bible Concordance*, Third Edition. Zondervan Academic, 2015. G1711, *ekklesia*.

[4] John R.Kohlenberger III, *The NIV Exhaustive Bible Concordance: A Better Strong's Bible Concordance*, Third Edition. Zondervan Academic, 2015. G3126, *koinonia*.

[5] Wilkinson & Finkbeiner Family Law Attorneys. "Divorce Statistics: Over 115 Studies, Facts and Rates for 2020." https://www.wf-lawyers.com/divorce-statistics-and-facts/.

[6] Gretchen Livingston, "About one-third of U.S. children are living with an unmarried parent." Pew Research Center. April 27, 2018. https://www.pewresearch.org/fact-tank/2018/04/27/about-one-third-of-u-s-children-are-living-with-an-unmarried-parent/.

[7] John Macarthur, SearchQuotes, November 22, 2021. https://www.searchquotes.com/quotes/author/John_Macarthur/

[8] Martyn Lloyd-Jones, *Studies in the Sermon on the Mount*, second edition. (Grand Rapids: Eerdmans, 1976).

Made in the USA
Las Vegas, NV
08 January 2022

40858746R00070